Connecting to The Word

The Word

Letting the Gospel Change Our Lives

Deacon Ron Tocci, MA Theo
with
Carrie Anne Tocci, MA, EdM

To Claire, With God's Peace & Blessings, Deacon Ron

XULON PRESS

Copyright © 2006 by Ronald J. Tocci

Connecting To The Word
By Deacon Ronald J. Tocci with Carrie Anne Tocci

Printed in the United States of America

ISBN 1-59781-957-3

All rights reserved solely by the author. The author guarantees all contents are original and do not infringe upon the legal rights of any other person or work. No part of this book may be reproduced in any form without the permission of the author. The views expressed in this book are not necessarily those of the publisher.

Unless otherwise indicated, Scripture quotes are taken from the NEW AMERICAN BIBLE WITH REVISED NEW TESTAMENT, Copyright © 1986 by the Confraternity of Christian Doctrine, Washington, DC. All rights reserved.

www.xulonpress.com

This work is dedicated to the memory of Ron Bosch who gently prodded me to write this book, and who certainly let his life be guided by the Gospel.

TABLE OF CONTENTS

SPECIAL LITURGIES

FOREWARD

Dear Reader:

I cannot introduce you to my father's homilies without mention of his spiritual bond to my mother. Two special portraits set in a single frame atop our living room mantle illustrate their predestined connection. On one side of the frame there is a portrait of my mother and on the other side one of my father. They are each in white communion outfits holding a rosary and bible in front of the very same statue of the blessed Virgin Mary. These portraits were taken separately on the same day at St. Mary of Mount Carmel parish in Utica, New York. Little did these angelically placed second graders know that years later they would stand together at the altar of matrimony to receive the sacramental blessings of the Holy Spirit in unison. Since that day, in my opinion, the Holy Spirit has been present throughout my parents' forty-two year marriage, and it was my mother's steadfast faith that led my father to his diaconal calling.

Prior to his ordination in 1994 my father was a college professor and textbook author, a committed husband, and a father to three adult children. Even though he had dedicated almost twenty-five years to teaching at Monroe Community College, he felt he wasn't helping people enough. And, so, with the support of my mother Catherine and the *Church of the Assumption of Our Lady* parish in Fairport, New York, he entered diaconal formation in 1990. Once ordained, he quickly transferred his technical writing skills to homiletics. Eventually, it became clear that his homilies should be shared with a larger audience. After years of thought, reluctance, and prodding, my father finally agreed to compile a number of his homilies into a book format. At that time, he asked me if I would write reflection questions for each of the homilies included in the book. I was honored that he asked me to help with this project.

You should know that I am a reader just like you. Since setting out on my own from Fairport and Assumption parish in 1988, it has become clear to me that we Westerners live within generally patriarchal systems and that the Catholic Church has been organized accordingly. Therefore, it was especially meaningful to me that my father chose a woman's eye, his daughter's eye, to create reflective questions for his homilies. I am a trained teacher and poet, and, therefore, have approached each homily as if it were a literary text. The reflection questions come from my own attempts to make connections with my father's words, words drawn from his life experience and his "everyman" spirituality. I hope our collaboration helps you to grow in your faith as it brings you in closer communion with God and with everyone whose path you cross on God's good earth.

Much peace to you,

Carrie Anne Tocci
EdM, Teachers College, Columbia University
MA, City College of New York
BA, Fordham University

PREFACE

I want to start by making it clear that even though this book is a collection of selected homilies, it is not aimed principally at preachers, those entrusted with breaking open the Word of God for their congregations. Certainly, I hope that the material in this book can benefit anyone who has that awesome responsibility. My intended audience, however, is much wider. It includes anyone who is seeking in God's Word some connections to the nitty-gritty of their lives. That's what a good homily or sermon is supposed to do. It is my wish that readers will find such connections in one or more of my homilies, and in doing so, will become more aware of the transforming power of God's Word.

All of the homilies presented here were written to be delivered at a Sunday liturgy. In other words, they were meant to be preached to a live congregation after the day's Scripture readings have been proclaimed. I strongly suggest that before reading any of the homilies, you first read the indicated Scripture passages, especially those that appear in **boldface** type. Then, read the homily as if it were being delivered from the pulpit, even going so far as to imagine the inflections and emphases in the preacher's voice. This should give you more of the feel of having God's Word opened up and laid out for you as it should be done every Sunday. You may even want to read it a second time — something you never get a chance to do in church.

Hear Me Buzz!

Someplace I heard it said that there are two kinds of preachers. There are those who are like *spiders;* they craft their homilies/sermons from that which comes from within. And there are those who are like *bees;* they craft their homilies/sermons by gathering nectar from other sources. I am definitely a bee! Much of what I incorporate into my homilies is drawn from a host of other preachers, thinkers and writers to whom I owe a great deal of thanks and gratitude. They provide the stimulus that I need to exercise my own creativity. Many of my homilies include ideas, expressions, and stories drawn from other sources which I develop, expand upon, and synthesize using my own creative touch. I add my own insights, experiences and stories, to create what I hope is a coherent and meaningful message for the people in the pews. Of course, the effectiveness of any homily depends primarily on the degree to which the Word of God is allowed to provide both the foundation and the inspiration for the message. During the process of preparing a homily, I constantly pray that what ends up on paper — and eventually comes from my lips — is the message God wants His people to hear through me.

As I said, preaching is an awesome responsibility. I am responsible both to God and to God's people. For some people, the Sunday liturgy may be the single significant connection they make with God all week. Many come hungering for something that will have meaning in their lives. It may be the only time they break away from the busy-ness and stress of everyday life to focus on 'God stuff.' Some may come to the liturgy weighed down with a problem, a hurt, a troubling situation, a question or confusion, hoping that maybe God's Word — proclaimed and preached — will speak to their need. Others may come with no specific need other than to worship with the faith community. They will listen to the preaching. They may or may not get something out of it. Either way, they are open to whatever way God wants to touch them. Then there are those whose only expectation of the homily is that it be kept short — the shorter the better. Even to this last group — maybe especially to them — the preacher bears an obligation to try to get through to them with whatever message God wants them to hear. Above all else, the homilist is one of the vehicles through which God tries to reach His people — even the ones who are not open to being reached. No preacher should ever take this role lightly or give it less than the best effort possible.

It's Not Always "Warm and Fuzzy"

The purpose of preaching is to bring God's Word alive, to let it resonate with peoples' lives, let it connect with where they are right now. Good preaching can help people cast off that which is weighing them down, that which keeps them from total union with God's will, that which prevents them from becoming all they are capable of becoming, all God created them to be. Good preaching can help to change attitudes and hearts to bring them more in harmony with the attitude and heart of Jesus. Good preaching can open people to new ways of seeing and thinking. It can lead them to a greater awareness that God's constant presence and power, God's love and care, God's mercy and forgiveness, are always there to draw upon when they walk out the church doors and return to the problems, worries, and responsibilities that are waiting in their world.

It must also be said that good preaching doesn't always have to make us feel good. A lot of the truth from the lips of Jesus isn't meant to make us FEEL good; it is meant to make us DO good. Sure, some of what He tells us makes us feel good. We can hear it in almost every church on every weekend. And that's okay; we need to hear these things to inspire us and encourage us to deal with the harsh realities of life. But church isn't a place we come to week after week simply to have our ears tickled. It should also be a place where we are confronted with the WHOLE truth of Jesus Christ — truth that cuts both ways. If you leave church happy every Sunday, something is wrong. If you leave doing spiritual cartwheels every week, something is wrong. Every now and then you should leave church crying, weeping, uncomfortable, maybe even angry because you heard the truth of Jesus Christ that challenged you to be better than you are, to stop doing some of the things you've been doing and stop thinking some of the things you've been thinking. That should happen in church too.

In my homilies, I have tried to achieve a good balance between the Good News that comforts us, reassures us, calms our fears, and the Good News that calls us to be better than we are. The overarching theme of all of my homilies can be summarized in my passionate belief: *God loves us just the way we are, but He loves us too much to want us to stay that way.*

Getting Personal

The homilies presented in this edition were selected to provide a diversity of themes and messages that can apply to almost everyone at any time. To aid you in making personal connections, each homily is accompanied by a series of reflection questions written by my daughter Carrie Anne. She composed these with very little input or guidance from me, so they come purely from the heart and mind of a reader just like yourself – albeit one with a very insightful eye (please excuse a little parental bias). Each set of reflection questions covers a number of different points or ideas from the homily, so you should be able to find at least one — if not more — that help you look more deeply to discover your personal connection to the Gospel message.

In Gratitude

Just some final words to acknowledge those who had a part in bringing this book to fruition. First, I am grateful to the many parishioners from the Church of the Assumption in Fairport, New York who constantly affirmed my preaching and encouraged me to publish my homilies. You have been very patient as I've dragged my feet for several years. I hope the finished product was worth waiting for. Next, I want to thank Carrie Anne for keeping after me to complete this writing project, and for her excellent job composing the reflection questions. Of course, it is unlikely that this book would have happened if God hadn't put Cathy in my life not only as my wife, but as a supportive spiritual companion. Finally, I give thanks to the One who made all of this possible by calling me to ordained ministry and giving me the privilege to proclaim and break open the Good News for His people. Lord, I hope that this little prayer that I silently recite each time I preach can be applied to the writings in this book:

"May the words from my lips and the meditations in all of our hearts be pleasing to you Oh Lord, our Rock, our Redeemer. AMEN."

Deacon Ronald J. Tocci
December, 2005

YEAR A

FIRST SUNDAY OF ADVENT - YEAR A

Isaiah 2:1-5; Romans 13;11-14; **Matthew 24:37-44**

Ready Or Not - Here I Come !

Today we celebrate the beginning of Advent, the beginning of a new Church year. The word Advent means "coming," and during Advent we celebrate and prepare for the Lord's coming. But there is often some confusion as to which "coming" we're talking about. In today's Gospel we are told "keep your eyes open, for you do not know on what day your Lord is coming." But doesn't our tradition tell us He is coming on Christmas day? No, that was His first coming, back there in little old Bethlehem (and it really wasn't on December 25). That's already happened…. And isn't He already here among us? Isn't that what we preachers keep saying? If He's here, then why are we still waiting for Him to come? And if He's not here yet, how should we prepare for His coming? We prepare for the Lord's coming by remembering and celebrating that He has already come, and by living in total awareness that He is with us now. So you see, He already came, He's coming again, and He's with us now. If you weren't confused before, you should be now.

Let's see if we can sort all of this out by looking at Advent in three stages: the past, the future, and the present. First, the past. During Advent we should prepare for Christmas by remembering Christmas past, but not JUST with our "business as usual" fanfare of presents and parties, tinsel and trees. We should look back more thoughtfully and gratefully on that day two millenia ago — on that most earth-shaking event in human history — that had never happened before, will never happen again, that turned the whole of history upside down. It blows the human mind if we just think about it.

Here's God — through His own Son, Jesus Christ — entering the world, not as an all-powerful God, not with the majesty of a King surrounded by armies and adored by millions. Instead, on a night we too often take for granted, He entered the world as each of us has entered it: out of a young woman's body, after nine months of feeding, growing, breathing, and moving. He entered the world in a forgotten corner of the globe, in a stable with only two humans there to see. We remember that night, not because it provides us with a charming story to tell our children about the Baby Jesus, but because from the moment Jesus took on our flesh, life would never be the same. That child grew into a man, a man who walked the dusty roads of Palestine, teaching and touching, caring and curing, showing us by His perfect example, how God had intended for human beings to live and love when He created us. And Jesus revealed to the world for the first time, God's unlimited love and forgiveness, through his ultimate act of love and forgiveness — the cross.

When we prepare for Christmas we can't remember what happened at Bethlehem without also remembering all that happened after that — from Bethlehem to Calvary to Easter, and all that is yet to happen. And that brings us to the future. In today's reading from Saint Paul and in Matthew's Gospel, the focus is on the future — Christ coming again. Words like the night is far spent, the day draws near," and "be prepared ... the Son of Man is coming when you least expect," warn us that Christ's coming at the end of the world or at the end of our lives — whichever comes first — may be closer than we think. The words of Jesus clearly challenge us to ask ourselves, "Am I ready; is my life where I want it to be when Christ comes?". Or are we like those people of Noah's generation who Jesus holds up as an example in today's Gospel? Are we caught up in the daily activities of life, complacently assuming that things will go on like this forever, that there will always be a tomorrow?

As I was preparing this homily, I came across an article written by a minister of a church in rural Georgia. In it he told how he and his wife had gone to the funeral of a relative of one of the members of their congregation. It was in a hot, crowded, little Baptist country church. As the coffin was wheeled in, the preacher began to preach. He was shouting and fuming and flailing his arms. "It's too late for Joe," he screamed. "He might have wanted to do this or that in life, but it's too late for him now. He's dead. It's all over for Joe. He might have wanted to straighten out his life, but he can't now. It's over.... But it ain't too late for you! People drop dead every day. So why wait? Now is the day for decision. Now is the time to make your life count for something. Give your life to Jesus!" {This must've been a great source of comfort to Joe's family.} After the funeral, on the way home, the minister who wrote the article said to his wife, "Can you imagine a preacher doing that to a grieving family? I've never heard anything so manipulating, cheap, and inappropriate. I would never preach a sermon like that." His wife agreed with him that what that preacher had done was terrible. But then she added, "Of course, it was terrible…but what he said was true."

She's right. In spite of his ranting and raving, that preacher's message is the same message we hear from Jesus today as He warns us that His coming could catch us off guard, totally unprepared. He warns us because He wants us to be ready and prepared when He comes for us. He doesn't want our life to slip away without doing the things we should be doing. He doesn't want us to come to the end, having been so involved with the busy-ness and the ordinary things of life that we kept putting off the more important things of life: the relationships we wanted to heal, but never got around to; the hugs we could've given but didn't; the words of love and support that went unsaid; those opportunities to share our faith with a brother or sister or spouse, that we let slip away; the works of charity we kept saying we'd do someday; the forgiveness we meant to give; the forgiveness we meant to ask for. The list can go on and on. During Advent, then, we not only remember the Christ who came to us in the past; we prepare for His coming in the future by living and loving as He showed us how to do — RIGHT NOW — in the present.

How do we do it? By staying awake to the ways Christ comes to us every day. He is here and alive among us even though our eyes do not see Him. He is here with us in this Church and wherever two or more of us come together to pray. He is here alive in Sacred Scripture, speaking to us as He did a moment ago, and whenever we take time to read the Bible. He is here alive on this altar in the transformed bread and wine. He is here alive within us when we receive His precious Body and Blood into our very own bodies. Think of it. Christ is here with us, within us. Advent every day!

If we are open and awake to the Christ who is here with us and within us, and if we let that inner Christ shine through for all the world to see — a world that desperately needs to see Christ — then when our time comes to meet the Lord, our friends and family won't have to face some insensitive preacher pounding on our coffin screaming, "It's too late for Joe!" or "It's too late for Mary!." Because we will have made our life count for something. We will have given our life to Him... AMEN!

CONNECTING TO THE WORD

1. How do you think the world would be different today if that first Christmas never happened ?

2. Are you distracted by the commercial symbols and trappings of Christmas? How can you redirect these to remind you that God became one of us?

3. This homily urges us to stay alive to the ways Christ is present to us every day. When you are caught up in the hectic pace of day-to-day living with so many responsibilities and projects and things to worry about, how can you stay connected to God? What are some ways you can be mindful of God's presence in your life? Are there any people in your life who keep Christ in your midst? If, so, how does he or she do this?

4. Near the end of the homily there is a list of some of the important things of life we are in danger of putting off until it is too late. Do any of these hit home? Could you add others to your personal list? Why do you think you might have a hard time getting these things done?

5. How does your inner Christ shine through? Do you let it shine through?
    When is it hardest for the Christ in you to come shining through?

SECOND SUNDAY OF ADVENT – YEAR A

Matthew 3:1-12

He's Pulling Into The Driveway!

"**J**ust wait 'til your father gets home!"….Sound familiar? I remember growing up how my younger brother Joey and I were a source of endless grief for our poor mother. If we weren't fighting or rough-housing, we were destroying the house with some kind of wall-rattling game like bedroom basketball or living-room hockey. "Just wait 'til your father gets home!" It seems like there was never a day when Mom didn't use this threat to try and get us to behave, and if that didn't work, she'd try, "Your father's gonna be here any minute!" That one usually got better results, but the one that really stopped us in our tracks was, "Your father's pulling into the driveway!" You never saw two little demons transform themselves into darling angels so quickly.

What's this got to do with today's gospel? Well, John the Baptist appears on the scene with a stern message. "Repent, for the kingdom of heaven is at hand!" As we read the remainder of the passage, we realize that John's preaching was certainly full of "fire and brimstone." His message was a kind of equivalent to, "Your father is pulling into the driveway!" It struck a nerve. It got results. Great numbers of people, even the religious leaders of the day, traveled the 20 miles or so into a desolate wilderness to listen to John's message of repentance and to be baptized by him.

All right. But this is the Advent season. Aren't we on the way to Bethlehem and the manger, Christmas, baby Jesus, Silent Night, peace on earth to people of good will and all that? What in the world does John the Baptist have to do with all this? On our way to the Christ-child, why do we need to hear this wild-eyed desert prophet shouting "Repent! Repent!" He and his message seem out of place in our celebration of Advent. "'Tis the season to be jolly." Who wants to hear all that talk about sin and repenting? We almost want to say to him, "Lighten up John! Don't be such an old Grinch! It's almost Christmas. We're trying to have fun here!"... But, every year at this time — on the second Sunday of Advent — the Church sticks old John in our faces to remind us that the original message wasn't "Christmas is coming!" It was, "Christ is coming!"

In one of our favorite carols we sing, "Joy to the world, the Lord is come.....Let every heart prepare Him room." That's essentially John's message to us. "Prepare the way of the Lord." Stop and take a good look at how you've been living, just as if Christ was "pulling into the driveway." Make room for Christ by clearing out all the bad stuff that keeps you from fully welcoming Him into your hearts, into your

30

lives, everything that keeps you from being all He wants you to be.

Now John wasn't wishy-washy about it. His sharp warnings about trees that do not bear good fruit being "cut down and thrown into the fire," and about the chaff burning in "unquenchable fire," suggest how serious God is about repentance. The repentance John preached was not a lukewarm, here-today-gone-tomorrow sorrow for sins. It was more than simply saying, "Lord, I'm sorry. I shouldn't have done that, now let me get on with my life." For John repentance meant a life-changing turn-around, a conversion, a recommitment to change the things we need to change. Not only do our hearts and minds have to change, but — as John stresses — that change has to be reflected in our behavior. Words alone won't cut it. He says we must "produce good fruit as evidence of repentance." In other words, "Our walk has to match our talk."

Of course, that's the hard part of repentance. When my daughter Carrie was very little, she got a sliver in her finger. I took her into the bathroom and got out the needle and the tweezers, some first-aid spray, and a Band-Aid. She looked at all of this and she didn't like what she saw. "Daddy, I just want the Band-Aid." she cried. Sometimes we are just like that. We come to God with our sin, but all we want is to cover it with a Band-Aid. We want to skip the treatment because we know it will sting. The treatment involves making changes, repairing any damage we have done, healing the hurts we may have caused, setting things right, and then making the commitment to let the Holy Spirit take over our lives and keep us moving in the right direction. That's repentance.

My friends, what happened on that first Christmas over two thousand years ago HAS to make a difference in what happens today. We can't let another Christmas come and go, put the decorations away, place the dried trees out on the curb, and have everything go back to how it was before. No, the miracle of Christmas — God coming to us where we are, God becoming one of us — has to make a difference in the world. And that difference can only begin with you and me. We get a better world by becoming better people. The world doesn't pollute our air or water. People do...The world doesn't fight senseless wars. People do...The world doesn't cause poverty. People do...The world doesn't foster hatred and prejudice. People do...The world can't fix its problems. Only people can — with God's help.

That's why the Church wants us to hear John's message year after year: "Prepare the way of the Lord...Repent! Repent!" because there's still time for us to make this Advent season different. We can make Advent more than mistletoe and malls, tinsel and trees, presents and parties. These are all well and good, but it has to be much more than that. We need to prepare for Christmas, for the Lord's coming, as if it's the most important thing in the world because it is.

We can make this Advent different. We can make this Christmas different. We can make them mean more if we would answer John's call to "prepare the way of the Lord...reform your lives." The events of September 11 and many tragic events since then, have been shocking reminders that our way of life, our sense of peace and security, can change in an instant. The only thing we can count on is the promise of Advent that we have a Lord who walks with us – Emmanuel, God here with us, even as we await His coming. And we must be guided by what He has revealed to us in His Word about seeking justice, about concern for the poor, and about the need to repent and to change our hearts, if peace on earth is to ever, ever have a chance.

So let's make room for the Lord. Let's clear a path for Him into our hearts. Let's get rid of everything that keeps us from making Christ the center of our lives. Let's sweep out all the bad habits and addictions. Let's throw away all our lame excuses, all our faulty attitudes and prejudices. Let's trash all the junk inside us that makes us hate and hurt and use and abuse others. Let's toss out all our selfish ways. If we would do that my friends, if we would do that, I can't think of any better birthday gift we could give the Christ-child. It would be a gift more precious to Him than all the gold, and frankincense and myrrh from all the wise men who ever lived. AMEN.

CONNECTING TO THE WORD

1. We are all Emmanuel's children. From your understanding of this scripture, what does He expect from His loved ones? Does He want our actions to be motivated by love or fear?

2. Are your Christian actions motivated by a "fire and brimstone" fear of hell and purgatory or are you motivated by Christ's promise of heaven, the home He has prepared for us?

3. What is your concept of Heaven? Can you do little things in your life to make your earthly experience more Heavenly?

4. Have you ever had a life-changing experience that has lead you to work for betterment in your self/community? Do you know any real-life angels, role-models who have motivated you to be a more loving parent, child, or friend?

5. What spiritual slivers have you humanly wanted to ignore or band-aid? What help is available to you, to help you pluck out the shards of hurt in your heart?

6. What can you eliminate to make space in your life for the Holy Family's healing love?

THIRD SUNDAY OF ADVENT – YEAR A

Isaiah 1-6,10; James 5:7-10; Matthew 11:2-11

He's The One!!!

Today we are exactly halfway through Advent, the time during which we prepare for the coming of our Savior, Jesus Christ, not only His coming as the cute little baby in the manger, but His Second coming at the end of the world. This morning we lit the rose-colored candle along with the purple ones. The rose-colored candle symbolizes rejoicing, rejoicing in the midst of the dark purple days of Advent, rejoicing because even as we longingly wait for Jesus Christ to come, we believe that He is already here with us. And this is reason for our hearts to be filled with joy, filled with hope, even those of us whose lives are not going so good right now. This is the hope-filled message that Isaiah sends to the Israelites in our first reading, encouraging them to take heart and not to despair as they suffered in exile. I want you to listen again to Isaiah promising the people what God would do for them. Listen and see if any of his words apply to you.

"Strengthen the hands that are feeble…Make firm the knees that are weak…Say to those whose hearts are frightened: Be strong, fear not!...Here is your God...He comes to save you...Then will the eyes of the blind be opened, the ears of the deaf be cleared...then will the lame leap like a stag, then the tongue of the mute will sing."

Do any of these promises apply to you? There is one that applies to all of us: "Here is your God...He comes to save you." He comes to save **you** personally. **You**. In **your** circumstances. And He comes **now**. This Advent. This year. This week. This day. This moment.The question each of us must ask is: what do I need saving from? How are my hands feeble? How are my knees weak? What are my fears? How have I been blind? What is it that I cannot hear? In what ways am I lame? What is it that keeps my heart and tongue from singing? What is there that I know I should change, but can't seem to on my own? How do I need God to save me?

Let's leave that question for a moment and consider another important question from the lips of John the Baptist. John's situation has changed dramatically from what it was in last week's Gospel. Then John was at the top of his game, preaching hell-fire and brimstone. People from all over the region were going out to him in the desert to receive his baptism of repentance, to prepare for the coming of the Messiah. Even the Jewish religious leaders went out to see what all the fuss was about, and John let them have it with quite a tongue lashing. But in today's Gospel, we find John, the dynamic preacher, the fearless, fiery prophet, languishing in a cell in King Herod's prison. Quite a drastic come down.

In his book , *Life of Christ*, Bishop Fulton Sheen says that John is discouraged and perhaps close to despair. He has spent his whole life waiting for the Messiah, and the last three years preparing the people for His coming. And now He has come – or so John thought – and where's John? Rotting in a dark, dirty dungeon wondering if he will ever get out. We find out later, that he did get out, but his body went out one door and his head out another.

Even though he was confined, John had gotten reports of what Jesus was doing and it sounded nothing like what he expected. John had been telling the people that the Messiah would come to bring God's fierce judgment upon the earth, vanquish the forces of evil and liberate the nation of Israel from Roman rule. But this Jesus wasn't doing any of these things. John must've agonized long and hard as he recalled baptizing Jesus, seeing the Holy Spirit descend on Him, hearing the voice from heaven saying, "This is my beloved Son." Jesus HAD to be the Messiah, but why wasn't He acting like one? Had John made a mistake? Was this really the Christ? He had to find out, so he sent two of his followers to ask Jesus, "Are you the One, or should we look for another?"

And what answer did Jesus give the messengers? Not a direct one, but a powerful one, one that sounds a lot like Isaiah in our first reading, "Go and tell John what you hear and see: the blind recover their sight, the lame walk, the deaf hear, the dead are raised, and the poor have the Good News preached to them."

Essentially, what Jesus said was, "Look around guys; see for yourself how people's lives are being changed because of who I am and what I am doing. Go back and tell John the kind of Messiah you see." Now, we're never told how John reacted to Jesus's answer, but for you and me, what's more important is our reaction. Because Jesus gives us the same answer whenever we — like John — are discouraged and on the edge of despair and we ask Him: "Are you the One or should I look elsewhere?" He says to us, "Look around. See how I've come to those who have let me into their lives. See how I've made their lives better. You don't have to look anywhere else."

That's what He's telling us: "I AM the One. You don't have to look anywhere else." Now I'll bet many of us here believe this. I believe it because I've seen the power of Jesus working in the lives of people dealing with some pretty tough stuff: a sudden, tragic death, a terminal disease, a marriage gone bad, no job and bills piling up, a spouse or parent who doesn't recognize them any more, a child facing a prison term, a severe eating disorder…just to name a few. I've seen them place their faith in Jesus, and call on His help. And I've seen how Jesus came to them, how He gave them strength when they were weak, courage when they were afraid, wisdom when they were confused, and peace when they were anxious. I've seen it over and over, so I know Jesus is the ONE. I know He is the answer. I know He is the solution. You know this too. Yet, how often do we look somewhere else for the solution to the problems in our life? How often do we try to find a solution in other people or things? How often do we live as if some other person or some other thing or some other idea is going to bring us the peace and happiness we never stop searching for?

My friends, if we haven't yet welcomed Christ, Emmanuel — the Lord who is with us — into our life, into our pain, into our joys, into every part of our life, then let's do it right now, right smack in the middle of Advent. Let's say to Him, "Lord, Jesus, I'm through looking elsewhere. You ARE the ONE. You are the ONE who can help me change what I need to change. Come into my life, Lord, into my heart, into my every thought and action so that every cell in my body, every molecule, every atom, every particle in my body, will bring glory and honor to You ." When we invite Jesus in, and let Him take charge — watch out! Our family and friends may not recognize us.

With Jesus in charge, we start to make changes in our lives. We discover we have the ability to make choices that are different than the ones we've been making for so long. Our behavior begins to change. We're friendlier. We're more positive, upbeat. We move closer to the front of the church and get deeper into the liturgy. We sing more, we pray more, we give more. We see beauty where we never noticed it before. We find that readings from Scripture begin to have more meaning for us; we find them having a real effect on how we think and act. Receiving communion becomes one of the most precious moments in our weekly – maybe even daily – lives. We take the Body of Christ into our own bodies with a smile on our face: "Happy are those who are called to His supper."

These things will happen. Not all at once. Not without setbacks or struggles or terrible trials. That's all part of it — just ask John the Baptist. And everything I've said to you today is what I needed to hear as well, so that together we can all say that here at the Church of the Assumption we have had the Good News preached to us, and that we have found the One we are looking for – or rather He has found us – and that we understand why even in the dark purple days of Advent, we light the rose-colored candle that tells us to REJOICE!, for our Lord is here with us. He has never really left. AMEN.

CONNECTING TO THE WORD

1. When you have been at the top of your game, have you stopped to reflect on Christ's presence in your life? Is so, where and how was Christ present?

2. When your game has become shaky, have you invited Christ into faltering areas of your life? This may seem like an abstract endeavor, so try to think a few concrete ways of doing this. Write them down. One way may be to simply ask Christ to enter your life, to ask for His guidance and help.

3. John questioned how a Savior should act. Imagine Christ in your mind. What does He look like? What is He doing? Listen to His words, the sound of His voice. Record how it feels to be close to Christ. The next time your life or your faith feels shaky, light a candle (perhaps a pink one) or imagine the light of Christ inside your heart.

4. Reflect on a recent liturgy that you have attended. Did you feel or sense Christ's presence at any point during the liturgy? Reflect on this moment. Does the recollection of this memory validate for you that Christ is the One?

THIRD SUNDAY OF LENT - YEAR A

*Exodus 17:3-7; Romans 5:1-2,5-8; **John 4:5-48***

How To Quench Our Thirst

The long story we just heard is typical of John's Gospel: it is packed with drama, dialog and multiple themes that would take me much more than my allotted ten minutes to unpack and apply to our lives. So I'm going to focus on just one of the main themes. I'll begin with a little story most of you parents can relate to. A father has just tucked his little boy into bed. Five minutes later, there's a small voice from the bedroom, "Da-ad...." "What?"…"I'm thirsty. Can you bring me a drink of water?"…"No. You had your chance. Go to sleep." Five minutes later, "Daaaad." …"WHAT?" …"I'm THIRSTY. Can I have a drink of water??".… "I told you NO! And if you ask me again, I'll come in there and spank you!" Five minutes later... "Da-aaaaaaad."… "WHAT?"…"When you come in to spank me, can you bring me a drink of water?" Now that's a thirsty little boy. And that's what I am going to talk about: *thirst.* Specifically, "How To Quench Our Thirst." Not our thirst for water, but the spiritual thirst, the spiritual longing deep in every human soul that cannot be quenched, cannot be satisfied except by the Living Water that Jesus offers us.

I believe that every human soul thirsts for, longs for, the same things. We long to be loved and accepted. We want others to see qualities in us that make them want to be with us, to do things with us, to really care about us. We long for happiness and peace; we know that problems and troubles and pain are part of life, but sometimes it seems we get more than our share. We long for meaning and purpose. We want our lives to count for something; we want to be appreciated. All too frequently, we try to satisfy these longings, these thirsts, by drinking up what the world around us serves up. We're taken in by what the mass media tells us are the best ways to find love and acceptance; we spend billions on what advertisers convince us we need in order to be happy, and we listen to Dr. Phil and Oprah to help us find meaning and purpose in our lives. I'm not saying these things are all bad. Some serve a useful purpose. But they're never enough. The result is that our thirst gets even greater and seems as though it can never be satisfied. In our Gospel, Jesus tells us – through His encounter with the Samaritan woman – how we can truly quench our thirst.

When the Samaritan woman came to the well for water that day, her world was way out of kilter. She had had five husbands. We don't know how those marriages ended, but it's likely that some of them had ended in divorce. Back then the decision to divorce was always the privilege of the man, so she must have been dumped several times. And now she was living with a man who wasn't her husband – a shameful situation in that time and place. It wouldn't be much of a stretch to surmise that she had a bad reputation and was something of an outcast in her community. Another clue is she came to the well during the hottest part of the day — when no one else would be there — probably to avoid the dirty looks and sharp tongues of the other townspeople.

So she came to the well not only with a thirst in her throat; she came with a thirst in her soul, longing for love and acceptance and happiness and meaning — and Jesus knew that. So He made her an offer. He didn't offer her natural water for her physical thirst; he offered her "living water" for her spiritual thirst: "The water that I give will become in you a spring welling up to eternal life." By eternal life, Jesus always means a life of peace, joy and content-ment that begins right now and will last forever. Later in John's Gospel, Jesus makes the same offer to the crowds: "Let anyone who thirsts come to me and drink. Whoever believes in me,...rivers of living water will flow from within him." (John 7:38). Jesus promises a life that is overflowing, a life in which every spiritual thirst is satisfied, to all who will come to Him, to all who believe in Him.

I would hope that most of us here believe in Jesus, are fascinated by Jesus, and feel some kind of longing for Jesus. But as we gather here today in His name, are we truly dedicated to Him? Does our being here signify that we acknowledge Jesus as the number one influence on everything we do? Are we so filled with wonder and awe at His being right here in our midst that we want to proclaim it and share it with others like the Samaritan woman did in our Gospel? Do we believe that everything we long for, dream for, thirst for, can only be found in a relationship with Jesus Christ, living by His teachings, and obeying His commands? Can any of us in this church stand up and say, "Yes! That's me. That's the way it is with me."? Are we drinking from His spring of living water?

As I was growing up, there were many Sundays in the hot summer when my family would pile into the car and drive to the local park. My favorite spot was this large slab of rock out of which bubbled wonderfully cool, crystal clear water. One family after another would come and fill up all the bottles and jugs they could carry, and it always amazed me that that spring never ran dry. You could stay there and watch bottles and jugs being filled all day and the water kept coming. That's how it is with Jesus. He's saying, "Don't drink what the world has to offer. It won't satisfy your thirst; you'll never get enough. Drink the living water I offer: believe in me, follow me, do what I command. It might be hard – even painful. It might be unpopular. It might be counter-cultural. But it will satisfy your thirst for good. It will be a flowing spring that never runs dry. "

My friends, do we realize how good God has been to us? He didn't create us and then leave us to figure things out on our own. God sent His Son to give us a clear picture of how to be fully alive, fully human, how to be the good, holy, wonderful persons He created us to be. And not only that, but God also made sure that it all got recorded in this book. *(holding up Bible).* Everything Jesus taught us is in here, in His Word. It's like this: First God gave us life, then He gave us Jesus to demonstrate the best way to live that life, and then He gave us this Owner's Manual for our life and said, "Everything you need to know to run your life the right way is in here. Something goes wrong in your life and you want to fix it, look in your Owner's Manual and you'll find the answer." Now I'm not very big on owner's manuals. Whether it's a car or a digital camera or a gas grill —whatever — if the owner's manual is more than a couple of pages, forget it. I'm not going to look at it. I'd never even buy something that came with a manual this big. Anything that requires all these pages to operate belongs at the NASA space center. But this Owner's Manual is different. Our lives depend on it, both this life and the next. This one we can't afford to ignore.

Many people say that the teachings and commandments of Jesus are too hard for most of us to follow. They're meant for the Mother Teresa's of the world. But as we read the Gospels, we can see that every time Jesus taught, He was speaking to ordinary people, weak, imperfect, sinful people like us – not saints. God would not have given us this Owner's Manual, this guide to living the fulfilled life, without also giving us the strength to live by it. And that strength comes from Christ himself, when we allow the Living Water He offers — His presence, His power, His Spirit, His love — to pour over us, to wash away our doubts, our resistance, our excuses, our distractions, everything that keeps us from getting serious about the Christian life.

As a Christian people, the time to get serious about the Christian life is always NOW. If you're waiting for a better time, there is no better time than now. In fact, Lent is the perfect time, the perfect time to immerse yourself in the Gospels, to reflect on them, to ask the Holy Spirit to help you apply them to your life. If you're in a RENEW group, you're already doing this with others who are serious about the Christian life. And when you do this, when you read and reflect on the teachings of Jesus, you will be amazed at what you will discover. You will discover what it means to be fully alive, to be whole and holy, what it means to be a good husband or a good wife, or a good child or a good parent, what it means to be a good neighbor, a good citizen, what it means to be a man or woman of Christ. AMEN.

CONNECTING TO THE WORD

1. Think of a time when you have felt empty or spiritually thirsty inside? Did you reach out to the material world to quench your thirst or the spiritual world? What or who did you reach out to first? Did this choice renew your spirit?

2. Have you ever thought of turning to Christ's Word when you are thirsty? As you have connected with the Word throughout this book was there a biblical reading or passage that was a spring of renewal for you? Mark these passages so you can easily visit them when you need to visit the well of Christ's word.

3. Recall a day when you felt spiritually quenched. In what ways did your actions on this day show that your wellspring was full and perhaps bubbling over with Christ's love?

4. Have you ever been drawn to someone because they have a wellspring of faith? When you have felt spiritually tapped, have you asked Christ to lead you to Him? Have you ever asked Him to lead you to a nourishing well of worshippers?

5. Have you ever reached out to someone in need of spiritual renewal? What led you to do so? How was your help received? What would you do differently next time?

SECOND SUNDAY OF EASTER - YEAR A

*Acts 2:42-47; 1Peter 1:3-9; **John 20:19-31***

Lord, Help This Goose to Fly!

What do you think would happen if you turned to the person next to you and said, "You know, I'm on a mission from God."? What kind of reaction do you think you'd get? They might roll their eyes, or try to move further down the pew, or pretend they didn't hear you. Or maybe they'd try to humor you by saying, "Oh, isn't that nice." In other words, they'd think you're some kind of wacko. Why is it such an outlandish notion that ordinary, real-life, everyday people can be on a mission from God? Could that kid checking out our groceries at Wegman's be on a mission from God? Could that elderly couple we pass on our walks through the village be on a mission from God? Could that annoying telemarketer who calls at dinner time be on a mission from God? How about that 14-year old daughter with her room full of giggling girlfriends, can they be on a mission from God? Can someone with bills to pay, kids to chauffeur, dinner to cook, a garage to clean out, and ten pounds to lose, be on a mission from God?

YES! All these people — people like us — can very well be on a mission from God. How can I dare make such a claim? Because God says so right here in today's Gospel. As we just heard, when the Risen Christ appeared to the frightened disciples locked in the upper room, the first words He said to them were, "Peace be with you. As the Father has sent me, so I send you." Then He breathed on them and said, "Receive the Holy Spirit." Here were these disciples who had abandoned Him, denied Him, misunderstood Him, and were generally clueless, and what did Jesus do? Did he scold them, rebuke them and tell them how disappointed He was in them? No! He commissioned them and empowered them with the Holy Spirit to go out and minister to the world. And from that moment forward, every one of us who has stood before the minister at our Confirmation and heard the words, "Peace be with you," and been anointed with Sacred Oil and received the Holy Spirit, every one of us — with the same human weaknesses as those first disciples — has also been sent out into the world. We are, indeed, on a mission from God. Because God, through Christ, has said so! "As the Father has sent me, so I send you."

You have a mission; I have a mission; Pope John Paul had a mission; Pope Benedict has a mission. We all have the same mission: to be Christ for others, to bring the love of Christ into our little corner of the world. We hear this over and over from the pulpit; we heard it whenever Pope John Paul spoke...especially when he addressed our young people. We know it's what God wants us to do. We're just not very good at doing it. Let me show you what I mean with a little parable. I've used it here before, but a good parable is meant to be used over and over.

It's about a congregation of geese: the First Geese Church of Christ. It was at their Sunday morning service, and the pastor waddled up to the pulpit and began his fiery sermon. "What kind of birds are we?" he asked. And the congregation answered, "Geese!" ... "That's right!" the pastor shot back. "We are geese! God made us geese to be geese, not ducks or sparrows or crows." ... "AMEN!" shouted the congregation, as they honked their approval. "And what are these things God has given us, these MAJESTIC append-ages?" ... "Wings!" they answered ... "And why did God give us these fine wings?" ... "To fly, pastor! We can fly with them!"

Now the preacher really started to heat up. "God WANTS us to fly. The moles can dig, the lions can hunt, but WE can fly! We can soar above the clouds! We can fill the skies. Praise the Lord! We can fly!"...."AMEN!" they shouted, "ALLELUIA!." Then the pastor challenged his flock, "If God wants us to fly, then what do we gotta do?"....."We gotta fly!" they yelled back ... "We gotta what?"..."We gotta fly!"...."What?"...."FLY!".... When the service was over as the congregation of geese were leaving the church, they remarked to one another how inspiring the pastor's sermon had been that morning. And then.....they all WALKED home.

You see what happens. Week after week we come here and listen as the Word of God is proclaimed and preached. Week after week we hear of God's incredible love for us, how Jesus sacrificed His life for us, and how He wants us to leave here after Mass and go out and love one another as He loved us. We may not respond by shouting AMENS or ALLELUIAS, but we nod our heads in agreement, or at least agree in our hearts that it's what we are being called to do. But, then, what often happens, is we're like those geese in the parable. We walk out of here no different than we were when we walked in. We leave here with no sense of being on a mission from God. Those geese were given the mission to fly — to soar above the clouds, to fill the skies — because that's what God made geese to do. We're given the mission to bring the love of the Risen Christ into the world, because that's what God made us to do. And we're the only ones who can do it.

Our Pope can make speeches and write encyclicals until the cows come home; bishops can confirm and ordain and punch out pastoral letters until the computer's bytes run out; priests can offer the Sacrifice of the Mass from dawn 'til dusk; deacons can teach and preach 'til their tongues fall off, but only you can bring Christ's love to your brothers and sisters out there in the real, day to day world where you live, where you work, where you play, where you shop, where you go to school, where you just hang out. When it comes to bringing Christ's love into the trenches, you are the frontline troops. That's your mission. And it's not an easy one, because the kind of love I'm talking about isn't the kind of love that has to do with emotions and feelings, like the love between husband and wife, or parents and children, or two sweethearts, or close friends. Jesus gave us a new standard for love — love that does not depend on feelings. Love that is not something we FEEL, it is something we DO...even when we don't feel very loving...

It is the love that Jesus says must be the identifying mark of all who believe in Him. In Greek it is called *agape'* which means unconditional, self-giving love, the love Jesus modeled for us, a foot-washing love, a laying-down-my-life-for-you brand of love, a putting-your-needs-before-mine kind of love. He said it very clearly: "You want to be my follower? You want others to know you belong to me? Then do for each other what I have done for you." Friends, it's that simple...and it's that hard. Agape', Christ's kind of love, says to a person, "You hurt me, and I'm angry enough to want to hurt you back, but I'm going to forgive you because that's the best way to keep this from getting worse." (Pope John Paul II modeled this so perfectly when he went into the prison cell of the man who had tried to kill him, and told him that he forgave him.) Agape', Christ's kind of love looks at a person of a different race or culture or social class and says, "I am going to treat you right even if I have to work through my ingrained prejudices and emotions." Christ's kind of love says, "I'm gonna give you help even if you don't deserve it, even if you don't thank me, even if I get nothing in return."

My friends, this is the love we have been commissioned to bring into the world. This is the love the world sorely needs — now more than ever. This is the love that can transform the world — one heart at a time. This is the mission we've been given by the Risen Christ: "As my Father sends me, so I send you." In a few moments as we come forward to receive Him in the Sacrament of His Body and Blood, let this be our prayer:

Lord Jesus, I accept this mission but I need your help. I can't do it alone. Fill me with your Holy Spirit as you did your disciples in that upper room before you sent them out. Lord, let your Spirit lift me higher than all the obstacles and barriers that have kept me from doing this up to now....Lord, help this goose to fly! AMEN!

CONNECTING TO THE WORD

1. When you leave church after the Celebration of Eucharist, do you take Christ's words home with you, or do you leave them in the pew? If you were a goose, would you walk home or fly home?

2. Do some of Jesus' teachings stick with you more than others? If so, reflect on why that is so.

3. What part of your experiences of being in church have the greatest impact on you?

4. Christ's mission was to sow the seeds of agape´. What conditions are needed for these seeds to grow and blossom? What could cause the seeds to remain dormant and never come to life?

5. Why is it hard to show agape´ to people who hurt us ? Forgiveness is a divine gift. How does Christ help us to offer this gift to ourselves and others?

6. Try to commit one morning, afternoon, or even twenty minutes to observing acts of agape´. Record and reflect on what you see.

7. Christ accomplished His mission on earth. Have you ever stopped to realize that He loves you so much that He has entrusted you with the mission of spreading His Word? Does this mission seem daunting or doable for you? In either case, let Christ lead you where He wants you to go.

5TH SUNDAY OF EASTER - YEAR A

Acts 6:1-7, Peter 2:4-9, **John 14:1-12**

Show Us The Father

Our Gospel passage takes place on that day in the lives of the disciples where everything is going wrong. Judas has just revealed that he's the one who will betray Jesus and has gone off to do it. The Jewish religious leaders are out to get Jesus and His followers; they want to get rid of them all. Peter has just been told that in the next twenty-four hours he will deny Jesus three times. And the real kicker is that Jesus has just told them that He's going to be leaving them. He has got to go. It was not one the disciples' best days. Even though Jesus tries to ease their fears with comforting words about His going ahead to prepare a place for them in His Father's house, words aren't enough — at least not for Philip. Philip wants more than words when he says to Jesus, "Show us the Father and it will be enough for us." Just give us a glimpse of God, and we'll be able to handle things after you're gone.

This request from Philip — who was probably speaking for the rest of the disciples — showed that they still didn't get it; they didn't grasp the connection between Jesus and the Father. We can almost picture Jesus shaking His head in exasperation and saying, "Uh, fellas can you get with the program? How can you ask me to show you the Father? What do you think I've been doing for the past three years? Let's go over this one more time. Maybe one of you should take notes. Whoever has seen me has seen the Father; my words are His words, my works are His works."

What He's telling them is that whenever they saw what He did for people, how He treated people, the sick, the hungry, the outcasts, the dregs of society, those who hated Him, even those who would kill Him, they were also seeing God. In everything He said and did, Jesus revealed the true character, the true nature of God. After He straightens them out on this, Jesus then tells the disciples something unbelievable. He tells them that if they believe in Him, they will not only do the things He did, but even greater things. In other words, after He's gone, people will be able to see and know what God is like by watching His followers and what they do, how they live. And that applies to each of us. If we are His followers, the world should see what God is like by how we live our lives. In order for God to shine through us for others to see and know, we first have to invite God in, invite God's Spirit into our heart, our mind, our body, our will.

Several years ago I discovered an ancient little prayer that does just that; it invites God to come alive inside of us. It's a prayer you would've learned on your mother's or father's knees if your family had been churchgoers in 16th century England. Here it is:

God be in my head and in my understanding;
God be in my eyes and in my looking;   God
be in my mouth and in my speaking; God be
in my heart and in my thinking.[1]

Before we can pray this prayer and really mean it, if we really want it to come true, we need to uncover what it is saying. So I'm going to put you to work this morning with a little spiritual exercise using this ancient prayer one line at a time.

God be in my head and in my understanding. I want you to think of someone you just don't understand. Bring to mind someone whose behavior just baffles you; no matter how hard you try, you can't understand them. We all have someone like this, so don't tell me after Mass that you couldn't think of anyone; I'll call you a liar. Think of that meddling or obnoxious person where you work who more than anything in the world you wish would get canned. Think of the child you're raising or that parent who's driving you crazy. Think of some group of people that you just shake your head at and wonder, "How in the world can they act like that?" Now with this person or group in mind, silently repeat this prayer: *God be in my head and in my understanding.* What would happen if this prayer came true? How would you see that co-worker, that kid you're raising, that parent, or that group you can't stomach? You would see them as marvelous children of God whose fears are the same as your fears, whose hearts are filled with the same yearnings and hopes that you have. If this prayer came true, we would go looking to find out what we don't know about each other — about each other's world — so that we could be more accepting and understanding. *God be in my head and in my understanding.*

God be in my eyes and in my looking. I want you to conjure up in your mind something that's hard for you to look at. Maybe it's someone you need to visit, someone you have loved or been close to, but now the ravages of age or the devastating effects of disease have made it hard for you to visit and look at them. Maybe it's an image you've seen on the nightly news like the bloated bellies of starving children, or homeless men urinating outside the Open Door Mission, or an angry mob burning the American flag. Whatever it is, hold that troubling image in your mind. Then pray, *God be in my eyes and in my looking.*.What would happen if this prayer came true? What would happen when you gazed into the face of human need? You would be able to look past the dirt and the ugliness, past the pain and the anger to see the face of Jesus. *God be in my eyes and in my looking.*

God be in my mouth and in my speaking. Imagine that you're in the office, or on the golf course, or in the cafeteria, and you've got a really good racist or sexist joke that you just know will get a huge laugh. Or visualize yourself on the phone with someone, and you've got a juicy piece of gossip. You don't know if it's completely true, but man is it juicy. Or you're having a heated argument with someone you really care about, and you're all set to lash out with the most hurtful thing you can think of to say. I want you to get those words right in your mouth — just about ready to spout them out. Now pray: *God be in my mouth and in my speaking.* What if this prayer came true? Where did those words go? All of those ugly words that we spew out and poison the air with? They're gone — vanished. *God be in my mouth and in my speaking.*

God be in my heart and in my thinking. Now I want you to go into the deep recesses of your heart, to that dark place Jesus tells us is the source of all our wicked designs, that place where the wrong kind of thinking can make us slaves to our prejudices, our jealously, our pride, and can even lead us to acts of violence or cruelty Go to that dark place and hold on to those misguided ideas for a moment as you pray: *God be in my heart and in my thinking.* What would happen if this prayer came true? Our hearts would be cleansed of all of that wrong kind of thinking; we would be motivated by only one thing — LOVE: our love for God and our love for one another. *God be in my heart and in my thinking.*

My friends, there are people out there — maybe even some in here — who are crying out, "Show me God, and it will be enough for me. Show me God and I'll make it through this." They need to see God, to know God's love in their lives, and we're the one's who can show God to them, who can make God real for them. By praying and living this ancient little prayer, God will be in our understanding, our looking, our speaking, and our thinking, so that others will see God through us, others will know God through us. May we keep this prayer always on our lips. AMEN.

CONNECTING TO THE WORD

1. Reflect on the ways in which Christ showed His Father's heart to others. What should they have learned about the nature of God from observing Jesus?

2. What are some of the ways we can show God to others in our day-to-day lives ?

3. Recall the times when you needed to have your mind and heart brought to focus on the things of God. Was there a relative or a family adage that helped bring your Christian heart and mind into focus?

4. Write down the words to the prayer from this homily, and put them in your pocket or wallet. When you find yourself in spiritual gridlock, repeat this prayer over and over. Note whether or not doing this serves as a turnkey to your Christian heart.

NOTES

1. This prayer and the accompanying reflections are drawn from a sermon preached by Thomas H. Troeger at the Chautaqua Institute in the summer of 1997.

SECOND SUNDAY IN ORDINARY TIME - YEAR A

*Isaiah 49:3,5-6; 1Corinthians 1:1-3; **John 1:29-34***

Chutzpah Or The Truth?

The other day I was thumbing through a book on Jewish humor, and I was amazed at how many words from the Yiddish language have become part of our culture. Words we might hear every day. Words like *klutz* — a person who has two left feet, is always bumping into or tripping over things. I use that one a lot. Another Yiddish word we often use is *schmaltzy* — you know when something is overly sentimental, like a schmaltzy movie or song. Another familiar one is *schmooze* — a lot of schmoozing goes on here before and after Mass. And then there's the word *tush* —– that part of your anatomy that'll start to wriggle in your pew if I talk for too long. But my favorite is the word *chutzpah*. I just like the way it sounds: *chutzpah*. A person with chutzpah is someone with a colossal nerve who does things that require a lot of gall, a lot of audacity. The book gave this classic example of chutzpah: a man who has been convicted of killing his mother and father, stands before the judge and pleads for mercy because, after all, he IS an orphan. That's chutzpah.

Now chutzpah can also be a positive quality as in the case of John the Baptist in today's Gospel. There was John standing in a group of people, pointing at Jesus, this ordinary looking man, this carpenter, and saying, "Look, there He is, the Lamb of God who takes away the sin of the world!" Did he really think anyone would believe him? Talk about chutzpah. Can't you just hear them? "John, you got some nerve, telling us this guy is gonna get rid of all the sin and evil in the world. He doesn't look like much of a fighter to us." Well, maybe they were right. After all, when Jesus came into the world, tyrants ruled the land, tax collectors were gouging the people, and the poor were despised and oppressed. After Jesus left, tyrants still ruled the land, tax collectors were still gouging the people, and the poor were still despised and oppressed. The world hadn't changed. So, was John wrong? Was it all just chutzpah? Well, I can't tell you the details of how one day the Lamb of God will cleanse the entire world of murder and rape, cheating and corruption, war and terrorism, child abuse and all the other evils, but the Bible tells us it will happen. Just look in Chapter 6 of Revelation, or in Chapter 17 where it foretells of the Lamb battling and defeating the forces of evil. We may not know when or how, but Jesus the Lamb of God will someday cleanse all of creation from sin.

But what about here and now? Do those words — "Behold the Lamb of God who takes away the sin of the world" — have any meaning for us today

— right now? They sure do! In putting those words on the lips of John the Baptist, the gospel writer was identifying Jesus with the sacrificial Passover lamb of Jewish tradition and Isaiah's prophecy of the suffering servant — an innocent lamb led to the slaughter for our sins. Jesus would become the sacrificial lamb, shedding His blood on the cross, taking the punishment in our place, making it possible for us to be forgiven. If not for the Lamb of God, our sins would separate us from God forever. There's no way we would deserve heaven.

Now some may ask, "Couldn't God have done that another way? Why did He have to send His Son to suffer and die on the cross?" Well, I'm not one to tell God what He should do, or shouldn't do, and no one knows for certain why God chose that way, but I believe that God did it that way — at least in part — to let us know: (1) that sin is a serious thing; and (2) that He loves us deeply. All the lecturing and preaching in the world couldn't get those two points across to humanity like the sacrifice of Jesus on the cross. We can ignore many things, but we can't ignore the Son of God on the cross.

And so for twenty centuries we have memorialized Christ's sacrifice at every Mass. And at every Mass we echo the words of John as we pray this prayer: *Lamb of God you take away the sins of the world, have mercy on us. Lamb of God you take away the sins of the world, have mercy on us. Lamb of God who you take away the sins of the world, grant us peace.* Then just before communion, the priest raises the Body of Christ and proclaims: *This is the Lamb of*

God who takes away the sin of the world. Happy are those who are called to His supper. And we respond, "Lord I am not worthy to receive you, but only say the word and I shall be healed."

When we make this response, do we really mean it? Or has it become an automatic response, something routine that we do without any thought or feeling? Think about it. There in the priest's hand — in the simple form of a wafer — is the same Jesus Christ who stood before John that day, the same Lamb of God, ready to grant us the healing we are asking for, ready to forgive the sins that make us unworthy to receive Him. Whether or not that actually happens depends on us. We have to really mean those words we say; we have to admit our sins, hand them over to Jesus and ask for forgiveness.

Now to speak about admitting our sins is to be somewhat "out of touch" with our supposedly "enlightened" modern culture. Because "sin" implies accountability or blame, and these days many people find it hard to accept responsibility for their actions, for the choices they make. They don't sin, they just make mistakes. They aren't sinful, they're just poorly adjusted, or they're doing what others have done to them, or they're only doing what everyone else does. But the Bible and the Church are old-fashioned. They teach that any willful transgression of God's commandments is a sin. And when we downplay or deny our sinfulness, when we act as though we have no sins that need forgiving, then we are saying that we have no need for Jesus Christ, the Lamb of God.

He's irrelevant. He went through all that suffering for nothing.

There's an old story about the time Emperor Frederick the Great visited Potsdam Prison. As he spoke with the prisoners, each man claimed to be innocent. Each one blamed somebody else or their circumstances or the system, except for this one man. He surprised the emperor when he said, "Your majesty, I deserve to be here. I'm guilty. No one is at fault but me." Hearing this, the emperor shouted for the prison warden: "Get this scoundrel out of this prison at once — before he corrupts all these innocent men." That man was set free because he admitted his guilt. That's how we will be set free. When we admit and confess that we have acted against God's way, we are freed to begin all over again with a clean slate — washed clean by the blood of the Lamb.

And after we have been freed from our sin and our guilt, then comes the hardest part of forgiveness – REPENTANCE....I know I told you this story before, but when my daughter Carrie was very little, she got a sliver in her finger. I took her into the bathroom and got out the needle and tweezers, some first-aid spray, and a Band-Aid. She looked at all of this, didn't like what she saw, and cried out, "Daddy, I just want the Band-Aid." Sometimes we are just like that. We come to Christ with our sin, but all we want is a Band-Aid. We want to skip the treatment because we know it can be painful. That treatment is repentance, which literally means a turning around, a change in direction. It's not enough to say "I'm sorry." Forgiveness demands change.

We have to change our ways, get our lives moving in the right direction so that we don't fall into the same old patterns of behavior that can harm our relationship with God, with others, and with ourselves. Jesus knows how hard this is; He knows we can't do it alone. That's why He's given us the Sacraments of Reconciliation and Eucharist. Strengthened by the grace of these sacraments, we can do the hard work of repentance, turn our back on sin, and let the Lamb of God transform our lives.

When we do, it's as if the old sins had never happened. God will forgive and forget as He promised in Jeremiah 31:34b: "I will forgive their evildoing and remember their sin no more." He will delete the files, erase the computer's memory. And if we fall again and we come to God seeking forgiveness, He won't pull out his clipboard and say, "Hmm, I've already forgiven you 316 times." God won't remember. And for that we should fall on our knees every day before the precious Lamb of God who came to take away your sins, my sins, the sins of the world. AMEN

CONNECTING TO THE WORD

1. After baptism, we are cleansed of original sin. However, keeping our souls clean is a challenge that lies at our spiritual core, that sacred place that must be maintained. Reflect on situations, acts, and decisions that have led you away from this sacred place.

2. William Blake wrote two poems that speak to the interplay between innocence — "The Lamb" — and experience — "The Tiger". When you have been faced with scenarios in life that want to devour your innocence, how have you responded? If you held on to your lamb-like innocence, how did you accomplish this?

3. If you chose to be devoured, how did you feel afterwards? Did someone else in your life make sacrifices to protect you from encountering harm again? Did you personally make any adjustments to keep ravenous sin at arm's length?

4. When we sin, we incur *spiritual* wounds that cannot be healed with antiseptic and a band-aid. We are all God's children, but when we reach adulthood we, like Emperor Frederick's honest prisoner, must come to terms with the sins we have committed against ourselves, our loved ones, and society at large. In what ways have you ever caused yourself spiritual harm? How did you repair it – if you did? Have you ever caused

another person spiritual harm? Did you repair it? If so, how did you do it?

5. God cannot forgive us if we do not forgive ourselves and those who have hurt us. Do you need to forgive yourself? Do you need to forgive someone else? Are you ready to be forgiven by God? Do your personal actions toward yourself and others convey a message of love and forgiveness?

6. To prevent pain in our lives, we need to give ourselves choices. Sometimes the best Christians do not realize that they have choices when they are faced with temptation or conflict. When you or someone in your life is in a seemingly choiceless place, have you sought advice or given advice that might prevent a painful outcome? If someone has come to you after they have made a painful choice, have you helped them manage their pain with compassionate listening? After you have been hurt, have your trusted another person enough to share the experience of pain with them? If so, reflect on if and how that sharing was helpful.

FOURTH SUNDAY OF ORDINARY TIME - YEAR A

Zepheniah 2:3, 3:12-13; 1Corinthians 1:26-31;
Matthew 5:1-12

We Are Blessed!

It was a warm, sunny autumn day, and an old man was strolling through a peaceful meadow, just savoring the beauty that was all around him. As he walked out of the meadow, he came upon a field of pumpkins growing on their tiny vines. He was a little tired, so he sat down to rest under an old oak tree, and he noticed that the ground was covered with acorns. As he looked at the pumpkins and the acorns, he thought to himself, "What could God have been thinking when he put these big pumpkins on such tiny vines, and these little acorns on such large branches?" After a while, he fell asleep. In the middle of his dreams, he was suddenly awakened by a falling acorn that plunked him right on the top of his head. The old man smiled as he realized, "Maybe God got it right. Little acorns are where they should be, and big pumpkins are in the right place."

God doesn't think like we do. God's mind doesn't work like ours. God's values are not the same as the world's values. Jesus tells us this over and over, and no more clearly and explicitly than in his Sermon on the Mount which begins with today's Gospel passage as he presents his disciples and the crowds with some surprising — even radical — ideas: *the Beatitudes.* As we hear these words from Jesus, we might wonder — like the old man under the oak tree — "What could Jesus be thinking? How can He associate blessedness and happiness with being poor, or sorrowing, or lowly or persecuted? If that's His idea of being blessed and happy, then maybe I'll settle for a life of unblessed and unhappy, thank you."

When Jesus said, "Blessed are you...," He was saying, "Congratulations! Rejoice!" He was saying there's something good, something beneficial about your situation. But what can be so good about being poor or hungry? Why should we be congratulated when our hearts are filled with sadness or sorrow? Since when is being lowly or being persecuted a reason to rejoice? Well, we could draw on all of the teachings of Jesus, especially His Sermon on the Mount, and try to shed light on what Jesus means in each of the eight Beatitudes, but I'd like to focus on just one of them — "Blessed are those who are sorrowing, they shall be comforted" — because it can apply to so many of us right now in our lives, as it has in the past, and most certainly will in what lies ahead.

The first thing to realize in this Beatitude and in all the Beatitudes is that Jesus wasn't only speaking in the future tense. He didn't just say "Hang in there if you're sad and hurting, things will get better by and by; someday God will reward you." He said,

"You are blessed RIGHT NOW, in the midst of your sorrow and pain." As you mourn the death of someone you love, or as you grieve over the breakup of your marriage, know that "You are blessed." When your body is ravaged by cancer, or when you are unemployed and out of money, know that "You are blessed." As you anguish over how to best care for an elderly parent, or when your heart is aching because your child has gone astray, "You are blessed." When you are saddened and distressed by the sinfulness that permeates our world, or by your own sins which threaten to separate you from God and neighbor, Jesus says, "In your sorrow, you are blessed." What Jesus is saying is that during times like these, when our hearts are heavy and we are hurting, there is something good about what's happening to us. But what on earth could Jesus mean by this? Maybe we need an acorn to fall on OUR heads.

Whatever else He meant, I think He at least meant this: that it's precisely in the midst of our troubles and sorrows, when we so often feel weak and powerless, that we are drawn closer to God, that God becomes more known and present to us. And if, in our sorrow, we turn to God, and reach out to God, then we are indeed blessed. As we come face to face with our human limitations, and realize how utterly dependent we are on God, on God's grace, on God's loving, caring presence, we are blessed.

Another way to look at this is that spiritual power lies at the bottom, not at the top. At the bottom, where people hurt, where troubles and trials and sorrows exhaust our human resources. When we're on top, when things are going great, when life is one good day after another, we tend to get satisfaction and meaning from the visible, material world and all that it values — power, prestige, possessions — and we find much less need for spiritual sustenance — for things like prayer, Scripture, the Sacraments. It's almost as if we say to God, "No thanks, I'm doing just fine thank you." But no one, when, or if, they get to the top, stays there for long. Life has a way of "bottoming" even the most self-sufficient and successful among us. I once heard it said that on the day President Kennedy was assassinated, a tearful Daniel Patrick Moynihan whispered, "When you're Irish, one of the first things you learn is that sooner or later the world will break your heart." I think it's safe to say that this pretty much holds true for the non-Irish as well.

Sooner or later, something from the bottom will come upon each of us. For some of us it will not come as traumatically as for others — but it will come — and in that coming lies a crucial choice. We can choose to expend our physical and emotional energy on things we can't control, on a futile search for answers: "Why did God let this happen?...What did I do to deserve this?" Or, we can recognize in our painful situation an invitation to turn it over to the Lord, to place our complete trust in the Lord's goodness, in the Lord's great love for us. The open arms of Christ await any who will come — but it's the troubled and brokenhearted who have the best chance of resting in His embrace. "Come to me all who are weary and heavy burdened and I will give you rest."

His arms are open wide as we lie in that hospital room, powerless and afraid, or as we stand in the doorway of that dark bedroom staring into an empty crib or empty bed. His arms are open wide as we receive one job rejection after another, or as we struggle to overcome depression and despair. His arms are open wide as we helplessly watch the life of someone we love slowly slip away. His arms are open wide when our family is being torn by anger, addiction or abuse. And they're open wide as we grieve over the injustice, the poverty and the violence that exist in our world and in our community.

"Blessed are those who are sorrowing, they shall be comforted." This may seem to most of the world as nothing more than wishful thinking, a sentimental delusion. But as Christians we know that in our darkest times, in the midst of all the trials and sorrows the world inflicts on us, we can grow closer to Christ. We can cling to Him more tightly and know Him more intimately, and draw strength from His love. And it's in the warmth and security of that love that we know what the world can never figure out - *we are blessed*. AMEN.

CONNECTING TO THE WORD

1. Has sorrow or grief ever caused you to feel separated from Christ's vine of unconditional love? At the time of your suffering, were you awakened to your blessedness? If so, in what ways? Or did you come to realize it only after your ordeal was over? If so, how?

2. In your experiences of sorrow or grief, were you aware of your original attachment to Christ's vine of love? Did the memory of your attachment give you security and the courage you needed to re-attach yourself to the vine? Did the church or fellow Christians help you back or did you do it mostly on your own ? What are some ways we might help each other to feel blessed during disconnected times of sorrow and grief ?

3. During times of pain and suffering, have you been angry with God? Did you think of Jesus' cry from the cross, "My God, my God, why have you forsaken me?" Which human emotions besides anger, do you think this cry contained ? How difficult is it to feel blessed when we are hurt and angry at God ? Try to think of some ways to help you be aware of your blessedness the next time you are hit by sorrow or grief.

4. What do you imagine is God's plan for your life? What is your plan for your life? Are there any similarities between these plans? Do you see

yourself and your life as blessed? If yes, why? If no, why not? How does suffering awaken us to God's plans for us?

5. Reread the beatitudes and, if moved to do so, reflect upon their meaning in your life. Which of the beatitudes have you known personally?

FIFTH SUNDAY OF ORDINARY TIME
- YEAR A

*Isaiah 58:7-10; 1Corinthian 2:1-5; **Matthew 5:13-16***

Into The Shadows

One of my favorite Christian writers, Max Lucado, has a wonderful way of spinning a story around a Gospel message to help it come alive. Here's one of his stories — slightly modified — to help today's Gospel message come alive.

Long ago — or maybe not so long ago — there was a tribe who lived in a cold dark cave. The cave dwellers would huddle together in the chill and the darkness, wailing and moaning because it was all they knew to do. The sounds in the cave were mournful and the spirit in the cave was death, but the people didn't know it, because they had never known joy; they had never known light. But then one day, they hear a voice from outside. "I've heard your cries. I've felt your chill and seen your darkness. I've come to help." The cave people are quiet. They had never heard this voice. Words of hope sound strange to their ears. "How do we know you have come to help?" The voice answers, "Trust me, I have what you need."

The cave dwellers peer through the darkness at the figure of the stranger. He is stacking something, then stooping down and stacking some more. "What are you doing?" one of them cries out. "What are you making?" another shouts. The visitor stands up, looks in the direction of the voices and repeats, "I have what you need." Then he turns to the pile at his feet and lights it. Wood ignites, flames erupt, and light fills the cave. The cave people cover their eyes in fear. "Put it out!" they demand. "It hurts to see it." "Light always hurts before it helps," he answers. "Open your eyes, you'll get used to it." But none of them will look.

The stranger stands next to the fire. "It's warm here. Do you prefer the cold and the darkness? Don't give in to your fears. Take a step of faith." For a long time no one speaks or moves. Then a figure slowly steps out of the cave toward the fire. "He's right, it is warmer … and I can open my eyes now. I can see." The fire-builder beckons her to come closer. She moves closer, extending her hands. "It's so warm!" As her chill begins to pass, she calls to her people, "Come out; come and feel the warmth." "Silence woman!" they shout from the cave. "Don't try to lead us into your foolishness. Go. And take your light with you."

She turns to the stranger. "Why won't they come?" she asks. "Because all they know is the chill and the darkness. They'd rather live in the cold and the dark than to change." The woman stands silent, looking first at the cave, then at the man, and he asks her, "Will you leave the fire?" "I can't," she answers, "I can't bear the cold, but I can't bear the thought of my people in darkness." "You don't have to," he assures her as he reaches into the fire and removes a burning stick. "Carry this to your people. Tell them the light is here and the light is warm. It is here for all who desire it." And she takes the small flame and steps into the shadows[1].

In today's Gospel, Jesus challenges His followers — and that includes you and me — to carry His light into the world, into the shadows. He's telling us that following Him is a lot more than simply coming to Him with our own needs; a lot more than simply coming to church to be passive receivers of God's gifts and grace. Following Him means bringing His light — the light of the Gospel we say we believe — to the cave dwellers in our midst. It means bringing His light to those living in darkness so that they might know the presence of God in their lives. All of us will have times when the Lord will plop someone down right into the middle of our life — someone He cares about deeply. Maybe it's someone who's lost their way, or someone whose life is falling apart. Maybe it's someone overwhelmed with guilt who doesn't believe God can forgive them, or someone with so much hardship and pain, they've lost faith in God's love. He plops them down in front of us, hands us a burning stick, and says, "Take the light to this one who is living in darkness and lead them to me." And sometimes we do it. But too often many of us don't feel that we're good enough or holy enough, or faithful enough. We might find ourselves thinking or saying: "What can I do, Lord? Send someone else !"

Father Milton Rudnick tells of a powerful experience he had while Pastor of a parish on New York's Lower East Side, an experience that reminded him of how God so often uses the most unlikely among us to shine His light for others. He tells of a 6-year old boy named Billy who didn't come to Sunday school often, but when he did, he was a disaster. Billy was nothing but trouble, constantly disrupting his class, talking out loud at the wrong times, leaving his seat to go punch other students. The teachers couldn't do anything with him and they were relieved on those Sundays when he didn't show up. Billy didn't have much going for him. He was from a very poor, broken home. He lived in a rundown tenement apartment. He was malnourished and he walked with a noticeable limp. All of this no doubt contributed to his obnoxious behavior.

Late one afternoon, the rectory doorbell rang. When the Pastor answered it, he was surprised to see

Billy there, holding the hand of a little girl about his age. "Billy, what are you doing here?" Billy replied, "Father, this is my friend, Celia. She doesn't know anything about Jesus, so I brought her here so that you could tell her about Him." The Pastor could hardly believe his ears. Here was this boy who they thought never listened or cared, bringing his little friend across some of the busiest streets in the city so he could introduce her to Jesus. The Pastor was so dumbfounded that without thinking, he said, "Billy, you know about Jesus. Why don't you tell her about Him?" The Pastor almost fell over when the little delinquent, with no hesitation and with total confidence, began to do just that.

"Celia, Jesus was the nicest person who ever lived. He was so good to everyone. If they were sick, He would make them better. If they were hungry, He would feed them. If they were sad, He would cheer them up. But some bad people hated Him, and one day they caught Him and they hurt Him and they killed him."... "I think I heard about that once," Celia interrupted. "They stuck arrows in him, didn't they?" She was probably thinking of the spear. Then Billy continued, "But you know what? He didn't have to let them do that to Him. He wasn't just a man. He was God, too, and He could've stopped them. But He didn't, and you know why, Celia? He did it for us, so that we would not have to be punished for the bad things that we do." This deeply moved the little girl, "Aw, he shouldn't have done that."..."But He didn't stay dead!" Billy explained. "Three days later He came back to life again. He went to see his friends and were they ever glad to see Him. Then after a while He went back to heaven, but you know what. He's still here anyway. We can't see Him, but He's here all the time. And when we're good it makes Him happy, and when we're bad it makes Him sad. But He'll forgive us if we are really sorry. And someday, Celia, He's coming back from heaven and we'll be able to see Him, and He's going to take us to be with Him forever. Isn't that wonderful?"[2]

As the Pastor took this all in, he marveled at how God was working through this child who never seemed to listen at Sunday school, who never seemed to care about the Lord or about others. And now here he was, so deeply concerned about his friend and her need to know about Jesus, that he did something about it. So the lesson for us is that when the Lord calls you or me to carry His light to one who is lost in darkness and we don't feel we're good enough, or holy enough, or faithful enough, we should remember Billy. Surely, if he could do it, so can we. AMEN.

CONNECTING TO THE WORD

1. Like the tribe in the cave, some of us create corners where we can hide from light. Have you ever hid in a cave? If so, what were you hiding from?

2. Identify areas or enclaves of darkness in your community. Is there any way that you can reach one individual who is living in the shadows of darkness?

3. Think back to when you were a child or a newcomer to the Christian faith. How was Jesus' life and mission explained to you? Is the recollection of your story similar to the one Billy told? Have life circumstances altered your relationship with Christ? How can you return to your first discovery of Christ? Can this first awareness be shared with others in simple acts of Christianity? Is there a person in your life who does not know about Jesus' story who could benefit from your sharing it with him or her?

4. How did Father Rudnick, Billy and Celia affirm one another? Have you ever been the receiver or giver of such affirmation?

5. Is it possible for all of us, no matter our age or education, to minister to others? If anyone has ministered to you recently, did you pass this gift on by ministering to someone else in darkness?

When someone reaches out to you, does it affirm that you too are holy and capable of passing on the gift of light? How does such an action affirm our collective Christian faith?

NOTES

1. This story taken from Max Lucado, *A Gentle Thunder* (Dallas:Word, 1995), 181.
2. Source of this story is unknown.

TENTH SUNDAY OF ORDINARY TIME – YEAR A

*Hosea 6:3-6, Romans 4:18-25; **Matthew 9:9-13***

Let's Get Jesus Out There!

I heard about this Episcopal priest in New York City who likes to take the Gospel message into the streets. He had a special tee-shirt made with a message on it in Greek taken from today's Gospel in which the Pharisees strongly criticize Jesus for hanging out with the wrong kind of people. The message was: "He eats and drinks with sinners." The priest would wear the tee-shirt and go into a bar. In almost every bar, someone would ask him what it meant, and when he told them, they would typically respond, "Well, if Jesus wants to eat and drink with sinners, He came to the right place."…But, you know, Jesus doesn't have to go to bars to find a crowd of sinners. Isn't that why He is here? St. Paul tells us in Romans 3:23: " For all have sinned, and come short of the glory of God." The fact that Jesus "eats and drinks with sinners," is fantastically good news for us. That's why He's here to share this sacred meal, this Eucharistic meal, Himself, with all of us who don't deserve it.

When we share a meal with others, there is usually more going on than drinking and eating. We talk. We listen. We laugh. We tell stories. We come away from the meal with more than a full stomach. This is especially true of the Eucharistic meal Jesus offers us today. It is a meal that has consequences… which I'll get to in a minute. It is also a very costly meal because it required a great sacrifice to prepare. Jesus gave His life to create this meal. When we take the bread, we are taking Jesus' body. When we take the wine, we are taking Jesus' blood. Jesus gave his life to prepare the feast of all feasts for us sinners.

Now many non-Catholics and — sadly — even a large number of Catholics do not believe that the bread and wine are really the Body and Blood of Christ. They say that the bread and wine are just symbols that remind us of the Body and Blood of Christ and help us to be more spiritually connected to Him. They say that when Jesus said at the Last Supper: "This is my body…This is my blood," He didn't mean it to be taken literally. They need to read and pray over John 6, especially from v. 51 on, where Jesus says over and over to the crowd that whoever eats His flesh and drinks His blood has eternal life. Then it says that many of Jesus' disciples found this too hard to accept, and they left Jesus and returned to their former lives. And Jesus let them go. Did He go after them and try to clear up their misunderstanding? "Hey, wait a minute guys, I didn't mean that literally. I'm using the bread and wine as symbols. They're not really my flesh and blood…Come on back. I need your help." No! Jesus didn't do that because He meant what He had said: "This is my body....This is my blood."

Our Church believes Jesus. It teaches that the bread and wine are truly transformed when the priest calls down the power of the Holy Spirit — transformed into the Body and Blood of Christ. He is truly present in the Eucharist. It still looks and tastes like bread and wine, just like it did at the Last Supper. Its appearance does not change, but its substance — the reality of what it is — does change. Somehow the flesh and blood of Jesus Christ are present in that wafer of bread and cup of wine. It's a miracle! God does miracles. Look at all those miracles Jesus did. Look at the miracle of the Resurrection. Look at the miracle of the universe. Look at the miracle of life, the miracle of your own consciousness and thought processes. Look at the miracle inside every cell in your body. The DNA code in a SINGLE cell is a zillion times more complex than your computer's operating system. This DNA didn't arrange itself by accident. If we can believe mighty God did all these things, then believing the bread and wine have become Jesus' Body and Blood should be easy.

OK, so Jesus is here in this Eucharistic meal, and like I said, this HOLY meal has consequences. Something more than eating and drinking happens when we come to receive the bread and wine believing they are the Body and Blood of Christ. When I respond "AMEN" after the communion minister says "Body of Christ, " I am saying, "YES, this IS the Body of Christ that I am taking into my own body." St. Paul expressed it so beautifully in his letter to the

Galatians: "It is no longer I who live; Christ lives in me!" When I come to communion prayerfully and worthily — free from any unconfessed serious sin — and I receive Christ, He becomes part of me; He lives in me! This boggles my mind. Why, should He come to me with all my faults and weaknesses and my hot and cold faith?

The answer is in today's Gospel. Jesus chose Matthew, a tax collector, a public sinner who betrayed and cheated his own people in order to line his pockets, and Jesus chose others whose resume's weren't exactly impressive either. He chose that sorry bunch to go out into the world and spread the Good News of salvation, of God's love and mercy. He chose them to be His presence in the world, and that's what He wants this sorry bunch to be — His presence in the world. That's why He comes to us in this miracle of the Eucharist and fills us with Himself, because there are places out there, people out there, who need Him, who need to see Jesus Christ, who need to experience Jesus Christ. My friends, if anyone asks you why you come to Mass, this should be your answer: "Because *Jesus is here...because J is here...and He wants to be out there*." Take a moment to think about what that means... *Jesus Christ is here, ...and He wants to be out there*.

It means that what happens out there is just as important as what happens in here. When Christ feeds us at this Eucharistic meal, He gives us this incredible, miraculous gift to strengthen and nourish us for our daily struggles. For some of us, these challenges are considerable. But that's only part of it. For baptized followers of Jesus, it's never just about "me." It's about bringing the Christ who comes to me in the Eucharist with me when I walk out that door, because *Jesus wants to be out there.* And He's counting on us to get Him there. Today's Gospel ends with Jesus quoting Hosea from our first reading, as He tells the Pharisees: "It is love that I want, not sacrifice." He's saying to them, "All the sacrifices you bring to the temple – money, livestock, crops from your field – mean nothing to God unless you love and care about your neighbor." What this says to us is that the sacrifices we make to support the church, and to be here and take part in this liturgy mean nothing unless we leave here and take the love of Christ that's within us to the people and places out there who need that love...*Jesus wants to be out there. And we're the ones who have got to bring Him there!*

Jesus wants to be in our homes, in our families, in the marketplace where we do business and in workplaces where we earn our daily bread. Let's bring Him there!

Jesus wants to be in our schools, on the school buses, on the playing fields, in the malls, everyplace young people spend time together. Let's bring Him there!

Jesus wants to be with all the lonely, all who are anxious or afraid, all who are on the edge of despair. Let's bring Him there!

Jesus wants to be with the poor and the vulnerable, all who need helping hands and hearts. Let's bring Him there!

Jesus wants to be with the aging, the sick, the dying, all who need caring and comforting. Let's bring Him there!

Jesus wants to be everywhere that racism, discrimination and prejudice keep us from addressing the needs of people and communities. Let's bring Him there!

Jesus wants to be everywhere that stubborn hearts refuse to forgive and be reconciled. Let's bring Him there!

Jesus wants to be everywhere that human life is considered inconvenient and dispensable. Let's bring Him there!

All right. I think we all get the idea. Let me end with the words of St. Teresa of Avila:

"Christ has no body on earth but yours, no hands but yours, no feet but yours. Yours are the eyes through which to look with Christ's compassion on the world. Yours are the feet with which He is to go about doing good. Yours are the hands with which He is to bless others now"

St. Teresa knew it. We know it. So let's do it. Let's bring Jesus where He wants to be; let's bring Him out there. AMEN!

CONNECTING TO THE WORD

1. Do you believe that the Body and Blood of Jesus Christ is truly present in the Eucharist? If not, what makes it hard for you to believe it?

2. If you do believe in the Real Presence, how would you explain your belief to someone who doesn't?

3. How or what do you feel as you go back into your pew after receiving the Eucharist? How long does that feeling last? Does any long-lasting transformation ever take place?

4. In your personal situation, what are some of the ways you can do better at bringing Christ out into your corner of the world?

30TH SUNDAY OF ORDINARY TIME
– YEAR A

Exodus 22:20-26; 1 Thessalonians 1:5-10;
Matthew 22:34-40

Doing Love

Based on the Gospel we just heard, I think Jesus should take over the IRS…Because I'll bet He could take those thousands of pages of tax laws — most of which are incomprehensible to the average tax payer — and reduce them down to just a couple of simple laws? Isn't that kind of what He does in our Gospel reading? When the Pharisees asked Him, "Which commandment is the greatest?", they weren't referring to just the Ten Commandments that God had given to Moses many centuries earlier. By the time of Jesus, the Jewish religious law had expanded to 613 distinct commandments covering all kinds of situations. Jesus stunned all of them by declaring that those 613 laws could be boiled down to one two-part commandment. We call it the *Great Commandment*: Love the Lord your God with all of your being, and love your neighbor as yourself. That's it. God's law is that simple. It's based on LOVE. God created humanity out of His abounding love, and all we need to do to live a life pleasing to God is to love God and love God's creations. It's that simple. We could put the whole Catholic Catechism on a business card.

As simple as it sounds, it's not that simple to do. For instance, how do I love God? As I was preparing this homily I realized that in all of my prayer and talking to God, I don't remember ever saying, "I love you, God." Maybe I had, but I couldn't recall it. So, how do I show my love for a God I can't see or hear or touch? Well, I ran across an essay by an 8-yr old boy that might shed light on the subject. Here's what he had to say about God:

"God's main job is making people... to put in place of the ones that die, so there'll be enough people to take care of things on earth...God only makes kids so He won't have to teach them how to walk and talk. He leaves that to moms and dads. I think it works out pretty good....God's second main job is listening to prayers. An awful lot of that goes on especially in church and at bedtime. God sees and hears everything and is everywhere. That keeps Him pretty busy...Jesus is God's son. He used to do all the hard work like walking on water and doing miracles and trying to teach people about God who really didn't want to learn. They finally got tired of Jesus preaching to them and they made Him die on the cross. But He was good and kind like His Father, and He told His Father they didn't know any better, and to forgive them, and God said, "OK!"...God liked everything His Son had done and all His hard work,

and He told Jesus He didn't have to go out on the road anymore. So He raised Jesus up to heaven and now He helps His Father out by listening to prayers. You can pray anytime you want and they will hear you because they worked it out so one of them is on duty all the time."

You know, that's pretty darn good theology for an 8-year old. God is our creator, God sees everything, hears everything, and is everywhere. God is good and kind and forgiving and is sure to hear our prayers because He's on duty all the time. Now that's a God we can love. But, again, how do we love God? When Jesus commands us to love God, what does He mean? Do we have to feel about God the way we feel about family and friends? You know, that warm feeling that wells up inside us and flows spontaneously from our heart? Like when a mom or dad hold their newborn baby for the first time or when a boy and girl look into each others eyes under a moonlit sky? We can't control those wonderful feelings. They just happen. Even Jesus can't command us to turn our feelings on and off.

The love Jesus is always talking about doesn't depend on how we feel about someone. It is a love that is completely in our control because it is something we choose to do, not something we feel. In Greek it's called *agape'* which means to choose to do good for another, to act for the well-being of another *regardless* of how we feel about them, just as Jesus, just as God, loves us — with no strings attached. For Jesus, love isn't what we feel, it's what we do.

We show our love for God by what we do for God. We show it by our prayer, by talking to and listening to God. We show it by how we participate in His Sacraments, especially Eucharist where we come together to praise and thank God for the gift of life and all the things God has given us to have and enjoy, and to receive His precious Body and Blood that help sustain and strengthen in life's trials and challenges. We love God by trusting completely in His love and care for us, not only on the days the sun is shining and birds are singing, but on those days when storm clouds gather and it can seem like God is far away.

Yet, we can receive communion every day, pray 100 times a day, say "thank you God" 1000 times a day, sing and shout praise to the Lord until our tongue falls off, and it won't mean a darn thing if we don't understand that the command to "Love the Lord your God" cannot be separated from the command to "Love your neighbor."…Jesus was the first Jewish rabbi to link the two together, saying there is an intimate relationship between our love for God and our love for all those made in God's image. There can't be one without the other. A good image to use here is a door. A door hangs from a pair of hinges. As long as both hinges are secure, the door will swing freely on the same right path as it was created to do. But if one of the hinges breaks, the door can no longer swing freely, and will eventually tear loose from the frame and become useless. In the same way, as long as we obey both parts of the Great Commandment — love God and love neighbor — our lives will stay on the right path God created us to walk. But if we choose to ignore either love, our relationship with God will eventually become unhinged.

1 John 4:20 makes the linkage very clear: "If anyone says they love God, but hates his brother (or sister), he is a liar." Jesus gave us the Great Commandment, NOT the Great Suggestion. If we belong to Jesus we have no choice — we have to love God and love our neighbor. We know from other parts of the Gospel that for Jesus "neighbor" means everybody and anybody. No one is excluded, not tax collectors, not prostitutes or lepers, not the one who betrayed Him, not even the soldiers who nailed Him to the cross. In a few weeks we'll hear Jesus describe how each of us at the Final Judgment will have to answer for how we treated Him in the way we treated our neighbor who was hungry or naked or sick or a stranger or in prison. Jesus always put a face on the neighbor He calls us to love, and the face isn't always pretty. It's the face of the annoying guy next door whose lawn mower wakes you up every Saturday morning. Or that boss or teacher or coach who won't stop making your life miserable. Or that sister-in-law whose politics make your blood boil. Or that dorky kid no one will sit with during lunch period. Or that obnoxious know-it-all who works in your office. The faces of the neighbors Jesus wants us to love include even the depraved faces we see on the TV news and the front pages: the drug dealers, the murderers, the sickos who prey on young children, the terrorists who slaughter innocent people. I'm sure you all have your own hard-to-love people you can add to this list.

It's a good thing Jesus didn't command us to LIKE our neighbor. There are some people we just won't ever like. But He did command us to love them with this strange kind of love — agape' — a conscious commitment to care for their well-being without any conditions, regardless of how we feel. So how do we do this? *How do we love the ones we don't even like?* By trying to understand at least some of what makes them tick, what makes them the way they are. *How do we love them?* By taking the first step to reconcile with them. Jesus told us "Reconcile with your brother or sister before you come to the altar." We have to take the first step. *How do we do love them?* By praying for them. Jesus told us, "Love your enemies... Pray for them." So we should pray that God will help them to change whatever it is that keeps them from being the way God wants them to be.

There's a saying that we should love the sinner but hate the sin. That may sound like religious jargon, but I personally know someone for whom I do that very thing. That someone is ME. There are times when I don't like me, when I really hate the things I've said or felt or done. But even when I don't like me, I still love me. I still want the best for me. I am still committed to my well-being. The way I love myself, I should also love my neighbor, even the neighbor I don't think deserves it, because that's how God loves me, and that's how God will know that I love Him...even though I forget to tell Him. AMEN.

CONNECTING TO THE WORD

1. When you look at yourself in the mirror do you see God? Who in your life do you love as you love yourself?

2. Think of all the people in your life that you put in the "impossible to love" category. What makes them so hard to love? Do you see anything of God in them? When they look at you, do you let God's love shine through?

3. When have you carried out actions of love in your life? Has love ever intervened to stop you from performing a malicious act such as gossiping or saying or doing something cruel?

4. Do you love the Lord your God with all your heart? With all you mind? With all of your soul? If you responded yes to any of the above questions, how do you do this? If you could not answer these profound questions, what are concrete ways you can begin to find answers ?

5. Have you felt God's unseen love in your life? If so how have you returned it to God? Where do you see God in this grasping, vengeful world?

6. Do you look at all people as your neighbors? Why or why not? Could you make greater strides to love your neighbors? How? Can your neighbors see in your actions the embodiment of the Good News?

CHRIST THE KING – YEAR A

*Ezekiel 34:11-12, 15-17; 1 Corinthians 15:20-26,
28; Matthew 25:31-46*

Tight Collars And Sweaty Palms

(Dear Reader: Before I delivered this homily, I arranged with one of the ushers to walk down the aisle toward the pulpit as I began preaching, and to pretend to have an urgent message for me. After he whispered it in my ear, I excused myself from the pulpit and went into the sacristy for about 90 seconds before returning.)

Today the Church celebrates the feast of Christ the King. Our readings present us .....Oh, excuse me. The usher is trying to get my attention......Excuse me a moment. I'll be right back............................ You are not going to believe this. I don't believe it. For some reason, Christ the King has chosen this church – our church – as the place where the Last Judgement is to take place. And He's back there in the chapel right now, and He wants us to line up single file to come and see Him — one at a time — to ask us only one question. But it's the FINAL JUDGMENT question....So, please, everybody line up.

What's the matter ? Doesn't anyone believe me ? You don't think it could happen this way ? Don't you remember Jesus' words in the last two Sundays' Gospels telling us that we wouldn't know the day nor the hour of His glorious return? Or maybe you do believe He's back there, or you're not quite sure, but you are in no big hurry to get in line. Of course, you don't see me breaking my neck to be first in line either. Maybe it's because we know from today's gospel what that final judgment question is going to be: "What have you done for the least of your brothers and sisters ?"

He's not going to ask: "How often did you pray? Did you go to Mass on Sundays? Did you read the Bible?" It's not because these things aren't important; they are. They help us to sustain and grow in our faith and grow closer to Christ; they help us face the challenges of living in a world where sin and suffering are very real. What Jesus is telling us in His graphic description of the Last Judgment, is that while these are all good and important parts of our relationship with God, the key element of that relationship has to be our love and concern for the "least" among us – the poor, the weak and the vulnerable, the lonely, the outcasts of the world. When we love them, we are loving God. It is by this that we will be judged. His words couldn't be any more clear. There's no way we can miss His point.

There's another point to His message: this love and concern for others must be more than mere sentimentality. We can sympathize with and say nice things about the needy, the homeless, the outcasts, but talk is cheap unless it is backed up by concrete actions like the ones He spelled out for us: feeding the hungry, clothing the naked, comforting the sick, visiting the prisoner, welcoming the stranger. Our love must take action; we must become involved in their lives, helping to improve their situation.

Now it seems that in spite of the great job of acting we just did, none of you believe that Christ the King is back there waiting to pass judgment on us. OK. You're right....this time. But that time is going to come when each of one us will stand face to face before the King. After hearing today's gospel, can you imagine what it's going to be like waiting in line to see Him? I wonder how many collars will be getting a little bit tight, how many palms a little sweaty, how many stomachs a little bit queasy. I once heard a popular Christian evangelist say, "If hearing the Gospel doesn't make you squirm, then you really haven't listened to it." On a squirm scale from one to ten, I'd say today's gospel rates at least an *eleven*.

Maybe I'm being being too tough on us. After all, I know of so many ways that people in our parish reach out to the needy in our community and beyond with acts of caring and compassion. There's our Social Ministry committee, our Sharing Program, our Stephen Ministers, visitation ministry and Kidz Kafe' ministry. And we have the folks who volunteer at Advent House hospice, Meals on Wheels, Fairport Baptist Home, and those who participate in projects like Habitat for Humanity and the Crop Walk. That's not all; there's also the Thanksgiving and Christmas baskets, the Christmas angel tree, the baby shower tree, the food and clothing collection baskets in our foyer which are always overflowing....I could go on and on. And on top of all of these organized efforts, there are so many people who quietly go about helping people in need without most of us knowing about it.

Yes, we are a caring and compassionate people. Yet, as our dear Fr. Charles Adams so often reminded us, we can never outdo God in our generosity. We can never begin to give to others in the same measure God has given to each one of us. We are all needy beggars, sustained only by God's grace, pure grace, nothing we earned or deserve. We must never get to the point where we think we do enough or that there's nothing more we can do.

Throughout Scripture, God is portrayed as having a special love and concern for the poor, the lowly, the outcasts, so much so that He sent His Son to live and move and minister among them. The judgment scene in our Gospel leaves little doubt that the acid test of our faith, of our love for God, is our love for these special ones of God. When we bring food to the hungry, when we give clothing and shelter to the cold and homeless, when we comfort the sick, when we visit those who are imprisoned or confined, whether in an institution or in their home. When we make the stranger, the foreigner, the immigrant feel welcome. When we stand against unfair discrimination of any kind. When we defend human life at all of its stages. When we do any of these, we do so because every life is a gift — a precious gift from God. We do it NOT because those we do it for deserve it or appreciate it or will be changed in character by it. We do it NOT because we want to be seen as a Christian do-gooder. We do it because our faith is a genuine, living faith and not just a bunch of words. It not just what we do here in church; it is not something we have like an insurance policy or suit of clothes. It is, deep down, who we are and how we are being formed by the Holy Spirit to become more and more like Christ .

This is how God wants us to be. This may not be how it is with some of us right now. But that's okay. That's why we are here at this Eucharistic celebration — to let the power of the Eucharist transform us, transform our hearts and attitudes, purge us of any cynicism or hardness or distrust than keeps us from becoming the loving, giving people God created us to be.

In a few moments we will come forward to reverently and lovingly take the broken body of Christ into ourselves. May we be as reverent and loving to all the broken Christs of the world. AMEN.

CONNECTING TO THE WORD

1. God so loved the world that He sent His only Son, and Christ loved us so much that He entrusted us with the world. How do you honor this trust as a caretaker of the world? How does your church offer leadership in your community's efforts to care for one another? Do you have any suggestions for improving these efforts?

2. God sent us Christ to be our model on earth. In your words, how do you hear Christ's message? Have you tried to follow his example? How did you feel when you succeeded? How did you feel when you failed?

3. If Christ is King, then we are his noble children. What are ways in which we can recognize this and treat one another accordingly? Do your actions acknowledge or ignore your neighbor's worth? What is gained when we build up people's spirits? What is lost when we break people's spirits? Looking around your community, where do you see a spirit of building, a spirit of breaking?

4. Another word for judgment is evaluation. Look within your heart. In what areas of your spirituality are you a needy beggar? When did this deprivation begin? Why did you ignore the pain of this lack? Is there a way to feed this part of your heart?

5. If you are in a healthy spiritual state, how did you get there? Are you in the position to help others to mend themselves? If so, how will you deliver your message of aid to your neighbor/community? What are spiritual tools that you possess that you are willing to share with others (e.g.., a rich prayer)

6. Spiritual well-being is an on-going process. We may see it in an individual before we see it in the greater community. After spiritual mending has taken place in an individual, how can the church community help the mended person maintain his/her wellness of soul?

YEAR B

SECOND SUNDAY OF ORDINARY TIME – YEAR B

1 Samuel 3:3-10,19; 1 Corinthians 6:13-15, 17-20;
John 1:35-42

Come And See

Picture this scene. A drunken bum has just finished a whole bottle of wine and is stumbling his way through the woods when he happens upon a baptism service taking place down by the river. He proceeds to stagger into the water and the minister notices him and says, "My Brother, are you ready to find Jesus?"..."Yah, preacher, sure."...The minister then dunks him under the water and pulls him right back up..."Have you found Jesus?"..."Nooo, I haven't!"... Again the minister dunks him under and pulls him up. "Brother, have you found Jesus?"..."Nooo, preacher, nooo." ...He dunks him under again and this time he holds him down a lot longer..."Have you found Jesus yet?"...Sputtering and spitting, the poor wino answers, "Nooo, Reverend. Are you sure He's down there?"

Brother have you found Jesus? When one really finds Jesus, it is a life-changing experience. In today's gospel, John the Baptist helps two of his followers find Jesus: "Behold the Lamb of God. There He is!" Jesus sees the two men following Him, and asks, "What are you looking for?" They respond by asking Jesus, "Where are you staying?" That's an odd response to Jesus' question...But a better translation of the original Greek says it means, "Where are you abiding?...Where do you stand?...What are you all about?" In other words, the two men want Jesus to tell them about Himself. They want to hang out with Him, get to know Him, know all about this man that John called the Lamb of God, this man John has been saying so much about. Jesus invites them, "Come and see." So they leave John and go with Jesus and from then on their lives are never the same.

Finding Jesus, following Jesus, getting to know Jesus, letting Him guide your life. Isn't this what being a Christian means? Yet, from what I've seen and experienced among Roman Catholic Christians — and this includes Church ministers as well the people in the pews — many of us seem to give more importance to the external parts of our religious faith than we do to our relationship with Jesus Christ. We frequently act as if Christianity is centered around the things we do and not around the One whom we are called to follow and worship and pattern our lives after. Too often we're concerned about the do's and the don'ts of our religion. It's like we're members of a club and we want to be sure we're obeying the rules and regulations. We worry about the rituals. Are we doing them right? Are we worshipping correctly? We spend a lot of time on programs and projects, committees and meetings, events and activities. Now all these things are good. They're all part of being a vibrant Church, but they can't change us internally. Only Jesus can do that. But only if we seek Him out, only if we put HIM before all these other things.

A couple of years ago in the *Catholic Courier* there was a two-page article about the Diocesan Youth Retreat that had just taken place. In the article there were quotes from interviews with teens and youth ministers who had attended and the Diocesan Director of Youth Ministry. Each of them spoke in glowing terms about the retreat and how great it was for the Catholic youth to come together to share in the marvelous activities and programs that had been put together for them. As I read the article, I couldn't help noticing that in the two whole pages describing their wonderful experiences, there was no mention of Jesus Christ — not once. I remember thinking that it could just as well have been an article on a Jewish or a Muslim Youth Retreat. Remember the slogan that candidates used in past elections to remind their opponents what the most important issue was? "It's the economy, stupid!" After I read that article I felt like shouting, "It's Jesus Christ, stupid!" I would hope that Jesus Christ was a big part of that retreat, but I sure couldn't tell.

Friends, when we start getting away from what Christianity really is, we need to go back to the basics, back to the beginning. I recall how the legendary football coach Vince Lombardi began training camp every year by addressing his players, veterans and rookies alike, and he'd say, "Gentlemen, this is a football." He started with the basics and that's what we need to do. "Ladies and gentlemen, this is Christianity." This is where it begins, not with rules and rituals and programs and projects; it begins with a PERSON — Jesus Christ — a very special person, human like us, yet one with God — the foundation, the cornerstone of our faith. Christianity is about knowing this person, this Jesus — not just knowing the details about Him, but knowing Him personally as our Lord and Savior. This is why He invites us as He invited Andrew and the other man in the gospel to "Come and see...Come and see what I'm all about."

Do you want to know what life is really about? Come and see. Want love and joy and hope and peace in your life? Come and see. Want forgiveness and a new start? Come and see. Want courage in your struggles and pain? Come and see. Want reassurance in your doubts and fears? Come and see. Want to find eternal life? Come and see. Jesus invites us to come and see not only for what He can do FOR us, but also for what He can do TO us. He alone can change us internally; He alone can change our hearts to be more like His.

Today, almost 40 years after the death of Martin Luther King who dreamed of and fought for a time when people would be judged by the content of their character and not by the color of their skin, there still are many Christians who harbor prejudice toward those who are different from themselves. Jesus invites them, "Come and see, and I will change your heart." Today, 33 years after our Supreme Court made abortion legal, 33 years after Roe v. Wade, after more than 40 million innocent unborn lives have been snuffed out in the womb, there are Christians - including many Roman Catholics - who see nothing wrong with abortion. Jesus says to them, "Come and see, and I will change your heart."

Today, 2000 years after God sent His Son, the greatest teacher who ever lived, to teach us the way of love and justice and peace, we have Christians who value profits and power more than they value people. We have Christians who see war as the best solution to global problems and not as a human tragedy to be used only as a last resort. Jesus says to them, "Come and see, and I will change your heart." Everyone of us has something in our heart that we know is not what God wants it to be. We know what it is. So to everyone of us, Jesus says, "Come and see, come and let me make your heart like mine."

Coming and seeing Jesus is a mystery. It's a mystery like this table around which we're gathered this morning. Christ Jesus is at this table too. It takes the eyes of faith to see Him, but He is here and He's welcoming us to come. Regardless of how we are feeling, regardless of what we are thinking, regardless of whether our faith is bright or dim at the moment, Jesus invites us to come. So as you come to eat and drink, listen for His personal invitation to you, listen for His words to you, and by now you know what words to listen for, don't you? ..."Come and see." AMEN

CONNECTING TO THE WORD

1. When is the last time you reflected on Jesus' character? How would you describe His character?

2. In your own words, who is Jesus, and what is His main message?

3. Is your current relationship with Jesus an active one, a passive one, or none at all?

4. Why do you think that many Catholics tend to place the person of Jesus on the outskirts of their faith development? Where do you place the person of Jesus in your faith development?

5. What can we learn from other faith traditions that teach us how to better our personal relationship with Christ?

6. What questions do you ask someone you want to know better? Have you asked these same questions of Jesus? How did He answer them?

7. What has Jesus called you to come and see? Have you shared it with anyone else? What more do you think Jesus wants you to come and see?

SIXTH SUNDAY OF ORDINARY TIME
– YEAR B

Leviticus 13:1-2,44-46; 1Corinthians 10:31-11:1;
Mark 1:40-45

Touching The Untouchables[1]

"**S**ticks and stones may break my bones, but names will never hurt me." I bet most of us learned this growing up — probably from our parents. It was supposed to be a way to protect ourselves against the inescapable teasing and name-calling of childhood. I remember using it quite a bit. But it never helped that much. No matter how boldly I shouted out the words of this little rhyme, it just didn't have the same power as the name-calling did. Names may not break bones, but they can sure bruise the soul; they can crush the spirit, hurtful names like: "sissy", "chicken", "geek", "fatso", "retard", "four-eyes." If we add all the four-letter words, racial and ethnic slurs, and sexual labels, there are plenty of ways to cut a person down.

I wonder how often the leper in today's gospel heard words like: "Unclean, unclean, go away. You're not welcome night or day!" How often had the leper seen children point at him and then scurry away? How often had he seen mothers cover their faces and fathers scoop up their children whenever he came into sight? How often had people looked at him as if he were a cockroach or a snake and crossed the road to avoid him? How often had he heard someone cursing him under their breath? How often had the leper repeated to himself, "Sticks and stones may break my bones, but names will never hurt me."? And how often had those words failed to stop the ache in his soul — the pain of being shunned and rejected?

The burden of all the insults and rejection had to weigh heavily on the leper as he approached Jesus. It was not only his skin that was scarred and deformed. His soul needed healing as much as his body. And so he got up the courage to kneel before Jesus — to take a risk that this rabbi he had heard so many good things about would not be repelled like the others, would not turn away. That was the poor man's hope as he begged Jesus, "Make me clean!"...Jesus did not turn away. Moved with pity, Jesus stretched out his hand and touched him. Then he uttered the words, "Be cleaned," and the disease vanished from the leper's body.

We might easily look at this as just another story of Jesus healing some poor unfortunate — just another miracle. If we did, we'd be missing the real miracle. Jesus had defied the religious laws, ignored the social taboos and had dared to touch this horribly diseased man. He touched the one everyone else found so repulsive and disgusting. We can only imagine that moment of touch, that instant when the leper felt the warmth of a human hand, a warmth he had probably given up hope of ever feeling again. That touch was the real miracle, the miracle that had lifted the leper's soul from the depths of hopelessness. With that touch, Jesus delivered a powerful message to this social outcast, this reject: You are NOT "untouchable." You are a human being. You are precious in God's eyes. You matter. You are no longer among the "walking dead." You are alive!

That powerful message is also for us because you and I have lepers all around us — people who are "untouchables" to us. In our second reading, St. Paul exhorts us to be imitators of Christ. If we are to be like Christ, we need to ask ourselves: are there people we prefer to keep at a distance; people who make us uncomfortable; people who we want nothing to do with? Is it because of how they look or the way they smell or the way they talk? Is it because of where they come from? Does it have to do with what they say they believe? Is it their lifestyle, the choices they've made? Is it someone in our family who has embarrassed us by getting involved in drugs or some other illegal activity or is shacking up with someone, or is gay? If we're honest, we all have to confess to having our own lepers — our own outcasts. Now the tough question: Are we willing to treat them the way Jesus did?

Some of you have heard me tell about Alfredo, a 12-yr old boy in Mexico whose story was on national television a few years ago. Alfredo had lost his entire family in a terrible fire two years earlier — a fire that had left his face horribly scarred and disfigured by the flames. Because he was so physically repulsive, no one took Alfredo in, and so he ended up living a miserable existence on the streets — on his own — living like an animal, scavenging for food.

One day, as he wandered through the city, Alfredo came across a home for boys — sort of an orphanage, but it was more than that. The priest who ran the home had created among the boys a real sense of family, a real sense of caring for one another. Everyday as Alfredo peered through the fence and watched the boys at play, he longed with all his heart that he could be one of them. After weeks of doing this, Alfredo gathered up enough courage to go and talk to the priest. When the priest saw Alfredo's face he was shocked, and when he heard his story he was moved with pity. But he didn't want to make the decision to accept Alfredo by himself. He wanted the boys in the home to be part of the decision. So he called them together one morning and told them about Alfredo and about Alfredo's desire to be one of them. He also told them that if they accepted Alfredo they would have to treat him as a brother. The worst thing they could do would be to accept him into their home and then ignore him or avoid him.

The priest then brought Alfredo in to meet the boys. As he stood before them, the TV camera captured the tense drama of the moment, scanning the faces of each of the boys and registering their horrified expressions as they stared at Alfredo's scarred and disfigured face. Then after what seemed like an eternity of silence, one of the boys stepped out of the ranks, went over to Alfredo, took his hand

and said, "You are my brother." With that, one by one, the other boys did the same[2].

Like that leper, Alfredo had also been a pariah, cut off from human contact, who was brought back into the human community when he was touched by Christ — Christ working through the hands and hearts of those boys at the orphanage. You see, that's how it works, folks. Christ depends on us to bring His radical love and His compassionate touch to today's lepers — today's outcasts. They will know Christ's love and Christ's touch only if we are willing to be Christ for them.

We gather here for Eucharist, week after week, and as we receive the Body and Blood of Christ into our own bodies, Christ becomes part of us; Christ lives in us. If we truly believe this, if it's not just some empty ritual we go through, if it's not some hocus-pocus we don't really buy into, if we truly believe we are carrying Christ within us when we go out that door, then for God's sake we have to carry that Christ out into the world. We have to bring His love and compassion to those who hunger for it, to all the lepers and the outcasts, both society's lepers and our own personal lepers. If we find this too hard to do, it's because there's a leper in us that needs to be healed first — that part of us we often fail to recognize — those fears...prejudices...hurts...blind-spots. We too need to come before Jesus and plead, "Lord, make me clean!" Recognizing the leper within ourselves, we will find the compassion to reach out to the leper in others. AMEN.

CONNECTING TO THE WORD

1. Have you ever felt like an outcast? Reflect on that experience. How were you treated? How did you feel? Did anyone reach out and touch you like Jesus touched the leper?

2. When was the last time you came into contact with one of society's "lepers"? How did you respond?

3. Have you ever used Christ's radical love to improve an outcast's life? How did it play out? Was it a win-win situation, the way it was for Alfredo and the community that welcomed him?

4. When you receive the Eucharist, do you feel that you are carrying Christ's love within you? Are you a tabernacle of His love? When you step out of church, when people meet you, do they see that you are emanating the light of Christ's love? Is it clear that He dwells within?

5. What are the lepers – if any – inside of you that need to be healed? Can these imperfections, if admitted openly, be confronted and healed?

NOTES

1. Some of the ideas and phrases used in this homily were drawn from an article by Thomas Troeger entitled *Preaching the Lesson* in the February 2000 issue of *Lectionary Homiletics*.
2. The story of Alfredo was taken from Mark Link's *Illustrated Sunday Homilies:CII* (Allen, Texas: Tabor Publishing, 1991), 77.

SIXTEENTH SUNDAY OF ORDINARY TIME – YEAR B

*Jeremiah 3:1-6, Ephesians 2:13-18, **Mark 6:30-34***

Finding Solitude And Silence

We all have people in our lives who depend on us: family, friends, our employer, our employees, our neighbors, our church. And that's OK. One of the ways we live out our Christian faith is by being there for those who depend on us. But there are times when we need a break from them. I once saw a cartoon that showed a pastor standing by a train that was filled with happy vacationers. They were all waving and shouting to him as the train pulled out of the station. The caption read: "It sure cost Fr. Joe a lot of money to send his entire parish on a vacation, but it was worth it." Kind of silly, but it made a point: We all need a break from people who depend on us.

Can you imagine something like this happening to you? You've taken a cruise to your favorite island paradise for a well-deserved vacation, and as you enter the hotel to check in, standing there in the middle of the lobby is a crowd of people from back home waiting to see you: relatives, friends, neighbors, your boss, co-workers, people from your church. And they've come all that way because they desperately need your help. Pretty unlikely. But isn't this what happened to Jesus and His disciples in today's Gospel? The disciples have just returned from the mission Jesus had sent them out on two by two, preaching, teaching and healing the sick. And they report to Jesus all they had done. They must've been feeling pretty good about what they had accomplished on their own, but they must've also felt physically and spiritually drained. So Jesus decides that He and His disciples need to get away for a while, away from the pressing crowds, to rest and to pray before continuing to minister to the people. But when they get to where they thought was a deserted place, this huge crowd of needy people is waiting for them. Jesus' plan for a time of peace and prayer wasn't going to happen.

Even though it didn't work out the way He wanted this time, the important point here is that Jesus knows something many of us haven't begun to grasp yet: we all - every now and then - need to get away from the crowds, the activities, the demands, the pressures of life to a quiet place to reflect, to pray, to get spiritually recharged, to let the reassuring love of God help us refocus on what our life is really about and where it is going. The Gospels show us that Jesus did this quite often. And that's what He's calling the disciples to do:"Come away...and rest a while." That invitation isn't only for those first disciples; it's for everyone, especially we Christians living in this hi-tech, hyper-speed society where you don't feel important or successful unless you're constantly busy and running from one activity to the next.

For Christians, it's not an option. We believe that Christ knows what's best for us, and if we want to stay connected to Him, if we want to keep our priorities aligned with what He wants for our lives, then we periodically need to break away from the world and find a quiet place to be alone with Him. Every now and then we need to spend time in SOLITUDE and SILENCE.

SOLITUDE and SILENCE: two things we don't get very much of in our culture. A culture in which we have to bring our laptop computers with us on vacation. We can't drive two blocks without talking on our cell phone. We work many more hours than 20 years ago. Our children's lives have to be filled with every activity and happening – they can't miss anything. The TV remote has become a permanent part of the human anatomy. Even when we celebrate Mass, we don't allow ourselves a minute or two of solitude and silence in the presence of the Eucharistic Christ. For many of us, seeking solitude and silence doesn't seem to be a very high priority.

But solitude and silence are good things. Solitude means we are alone. We turn off all activity, tune out all distractions. But we are not really alone, because in solitude is where we meet Jesus. He enters into our solitude, bringing fresh hope and insights into our lives and situations. He enters our solitude because we've made space for Him in our busy lives. We've said to Him, "Lord, my life is full of important things I should be doing, but right now being with you is

Connecting To The Word

more important." Solitude doesn't require a special place. For some people it's over a cup of coffee before the rest of the family gets up in the morning, or alone in a quiet room after the family is in bed. Others find it walking along the canal or in the car on the way to work. If we really want to spend time with our Savior, we'll find a place.

Just as we occasionally need solitude, we also need silence. We're surrounded by a cacophony of sounds and noises everyday that make it very hard for us to hear Jesus. We need the occasional oasis of silence — no music, no TV, no talking, just silence — so that we can listen to Him, let Him enter into our thoughts and hearts. In solitude we meet Jesus. In silence we hear Him.

If you're like me, the silence is a lot harder than the solitude, because silence is more than quiet surroundings; it's being quiet ourselves — both our minds and our mouths. If we want to hear what Jesus has to say, we can't be thinking about what to do for supper, or planning our to-do list for tomorrow, or have songs from our favorite CD running through our head. And we need to stop talking. One morning not long ago, I got up very early and went out on the deck. It was just me and the chirping birds and scurrying squirrels. The lawn mowers and weed whackers were still asleep. It was very peaceful. I began to pray in my usual fashion, telling Jesus about this tough situation I was dealing with, and how I wasn't handling it very well, and I needed His help to handle it better. As usual I was doing all the talking. I was asking for His help, but I wasn't taking the

132

time to listen. When I finally realized this, I said to myself, "Can't you shut up for a minute and listen? Jesus doesn't need you to tell Him what's going on. He knows what's going on. He's got things you need to hear. How can He help you if you won't shut up and listen?" So I emptied my mind, closed my mouth and listened. It wasn't easy for me, but I did it. When I did, Jesus came into my thoughts and my heart and I was able to hear what He wanted me to hear.

Last weekend at the Catholic Youth Conference in Steubenville, one of our young people, who had just come from a session on prayer, came to me and asked, "Deacon Ron, When I'm praying quietly and listening for Jesus, how do I know that what comes into my head is from Him and not just my own rambling thoughts? How can I tell when Jesus is communicating with me?" I told her that whenever we take the time to place ourselves in a state of solitude and silence, and invite Jesus into it, He will never refuse our invitation. In Scripture, the Lord says, "Seek me with all your heart, and you will find me." When we invite Him into our solitude and silence with all our heart, He will come. And if we are really listening, we will hear and recognize His voice. He told us we would when He said, "I am the Good Shepherd. My sheep hear my voice,...and they follow me." Hearing His voice in our heads and hearts, we will know what path He's telling us is the one we should follow. It may not be the one we expected, but we can be sure of this: it will be the path that takes us where we need to go. AMEN.

CONNECTING TO THE WORD

1. How do you respond when Jesus says, "Come away and rest a while?"

2. What is involved with making an appointment with someone? How would you go about making an appointment with Jesus?

3. Is the idea of allotting time for Jesus, an unlikely consideration for your daily schedule? If so, why?

4. Is your life congested with many obligations? If it is, do you prefer this gridlocked lifestyle? Or would you like to spend more time in quiet solitude in the company of Jesus?

5. What are some of the obligations and distractions that keep you from feeling Christ's closeness to you? Devise a plan that will free you up from some of them. Then try it.

TWENTY SEVENTH SUNDAY OF ORDINARY TIME – YEAR B

Genesis 2:18-24; Hebrews 2:9-11; Mark 10:2-16

What God Has Joined Together

"God created them, male and female... A man shall leave his father and mother and be joined to his wife, and the two shall become one flesh." We just heard Jesus quote these words from the very first book of the Bible to remind the Pharisees that God's original purpose in creating male and female was to bring them together in the unifying bond of marriage — the two becoming one. Jesus then adds His own words — words repeated at every Christian marriage ceremony: "What God has joined together, let no one divide." These clear, powerful words from the lips of Jesus leave little doubt where He stands on marriage. When God brings two people together, Jesus wants that marriage to last. He wants every marriage to be a permanent commitment to stick together — to stay together. You can call Jesus a cockeyed idealist, but that was God's intention from the beginning.

Yet we also know that from the beginning, fallen humanity has failed to carry out God's intentions,

God's vision of how the world should be. So, it's no surprise that even though almost every couple who gets married intends to stay together — at least that's the sacred promise they make during the wedding rite — marriage is not doing very well these days. It's in big trouble. The number of broken homes, broken families goes up every year. Still, despite the alarming statistics, there are many successful marriages — marriages that beat the odds, marriages that prove that Jesus' expectations are not unreasonable. Today's readings prompt us to take a look at just what makes for a successful marriage — what goes into making a marriage work. After 42 years of marriage (that's a long time to be married to the same person. Just ask my wife, she'll tell you), and after eleven years helping prepare couples for married life and listening to their thoughts and ideas, here's what I've come up with as the most important ingredients for a solid, lasting marriage.

First, there's love. Everyone knows "you gotta have love." But what kind of love? Is it that romantic, passionate love, that burning desire to be near each other all the time? Well, you do kind of need it in the beginning to get everything started, but as time goes on it's going to cool down. Now don't get me wrong, romantic love is great — I like it as much as the next guy — but it's not the kind of love that can sustain a marriage by itself over the long haul. For that we need a love that is more than just feelings and emotions which can come and go: "I love you today, tomorrow who knows." We need a love patterned after the love Jesus has for us, one in which we give of our self to the other, a self-giving love that doesn't vanish when the going gets tough, a love that doesn't see things as 50-50, but more like 70-30 or 80-20, with each partner giving more than they expect in return.

Let me give you a few examples in the words of 8-year old children who were asked to describe the love they see in their families: *Love is when Daddy makes coffee for Mommy and he takes a sip before giving it to her, to make sure the taste is OK...Love is when grandma got arthritis and she couldn't bend over to cut her toenails anymore. So grandpa does it for her all the time, even when his hands got arthritis too... Love is when Mommy gives Daddy the best piece of chicken*....(Here's my favorite) *Love is when Mommy sees Daddy on the toilet and she doesn't think it's gross*...There's a lesson here folks...Whatever our kids learn about married love, they don't learn from TV or movies; they learn from us.

Another important part of marriage is communication. Of course, we all know that when we're not talking and listening to each other, the marriage is in trouble. What we often fail to realize, though, is that what we don't say can be just as important as what we do say. The writer Ogden Nash put it more poetically: "To keep your marriage brimming, with love in the loving cup, if you're ever wrong admit it, if you're ever right shut up!"

Another thing we don't always get about communicating with our spouse is this: the most important words we ever say to each other are not the words, "I love you." Sure, these are important, but the most important words we say are, "I'm sorry," and "I forgive you." You might remember that line from the popular movie of the 70's: "Love means never having to say you're sorry." That's just a bunch of Hollywood drivel because marriage is a sacred promise made NOT between two saints, but between a man and a woman, two imperfect images of God who can at times be very self-centered and incredibly capable of hurting the one they love the most. There's no better way to strengthen a marriage than to follow the advice of St. Paul: "The Lord has forgiven you; now you must do the same."

This brings us to the next ingredient of a lasting marriage. Let me introduce it by describing a scene from a Thornton Wilder play called *The Skin of Our Teeth*. In that scene, a husband and wife, George and Maggie, are walking along the boardwalk in Atlantic City with their children. George has just come from having a somewhat flirty conversation with an attractive young woman named Sabina. After seeing this, Maggie says to her husband in a very calm voice, "I didn't marry you because you were perfect. I didn't even marry you because I loved you. I married you because you gave me a promise." Then as she looks at her wedding ring, she says, "That promise made up for your faults. The promise I gave you made up for mine. Two imperfect people got married and it was the promise that made the marriage. And when our children were growing up, it wasn't our house that protected them; it wasn't our love that protected them. It was that promise."

In that scene, Maggie zeros in on the one reality that separates marriage from every other human relationship: the PROMISE, the commitment, the sacred pledge made before God and witnesses to stick with each other no matter what happens — no matter what. Now it's easy to stick it out when times are good, when the refrigerator is full, when there are no bills you can't pay, when the kids are doing well in school and they have no problems, when everyone's health is good, when you love your job, when you're not exhausted and stressed out, when there's nobody else you're attracted to. Times like these, it's easy. But anyone who's been married knows there are going to be times that are not so good. There are going to be times when your commitment to each other will be tested, times when you don't feel like keeping the promises you made, when you may even be tempted to do as so many do today: "That's it. This marriage is over. I'm outta here!" Real commitment means recognizing that if your marriage is going to survive those troubled times, *God has to be at the center*.

There's the final piece, the most important ingredient in a successful marriage: GOD. Christian marriage is not a contract between two persons; it is a sacred covenant between three. As the man and woman pledge their undying love and faithfulness to each other before God and the Church, God makes this promise to them: "Put your hands in mine. Trust me as my own Son trusted me from Nazareth to Calvary. Plan and live your life together in prayerful oneness with me, and I will always be there to give you the courage and strength and the staying power to remain faithful to the promises you make today."

When a couple accepts God's invitation to make Him a partner in their marriage, the other elements will fall into place: love, communication, forgiveness, commitment. I'm not saying everything will be wonderful and perfect, that the Lord will flatten out all the hills and mountains that come along. What I am saying is He will be there to hold on to as the three of them climb those hills and mountains together.

I began with the powerful words of Jesus from today's gospel: "What God has joined together let no one divide." Let's take these words and make them positive instead of negative: What God has joined together, let all of us work to keep together. AMEN.

CONNECTING TO THE WORD

1. How do you define commitment? What people and/or organizations are you committed to? How do you maintain your commitment? What are the challenges of commitment? What are the benefits of commitment?

2. Do you take time to communicate with your loved one? Do you take time to speak with God? Do you make time to communicate with God; with your partner?

3. Reflect on your partner's perfections and imperfections. Reflect on your perfections and imperfections. Have your imperfections caused you to sin against yourself or others? Are you capable of receiving God's forgiveness when you hurt your loved ones? Are you capable of offering forgiveness to loved ones who have hurt you?

4. If you are married, are you and your partner living up to Christ's "stick together" expectations? If so, how? If you have separated or divorced from your spouse, what could you do to avoid this break in the future? Are you willing to let God be the glue that keeps you together?

5. Do you trust the covenant God made with us? Do you trust the covenant you have made with your loved ones? What aspects of your relationship (if any) are sacred? If there are none, why

not? Could a renewal of your vows reinvigorate the sacredness of your promise to one another?

6. How can married couples help themselves to stay together? How can we, the Church, help married couples stay together?

THIRTY-SECOND SUNDAY OF ORDINARY TIME – YEAR B

1Kings 17:10-16; Hebrews 9:24-28;
Mark 12:38-44

Keep On Pedaling

A pastor in Gary, Indiana tells this story. "Several years ago, a woman with two small children stopped to talk to me after a Sunday service. She told me she and her sons had been living in a battered women's shelter. They would be getting on a bus and leaving the next day to begin a new life in a new city, far away from her abusive husband. She talked about how hard it would be alone in a strange city, searching for a job and housing and getting herself on her feet, and how she was going to have to trust God if they were going to make it. She asked for the church to pray for her and her boys. Then she counted out exactly $30.56 and handed it to me. She explained that this was her tithe, ten percent of all that she had. I refused to take the money and said she and her sons needed it more than the church. But her response was clear, 'You don't understand, pastor. I want to give it to God. I trust that God will take care of us as we start our new life. To show Him I trust

Him, I want to give my share.'" The pastor went on to say that he never heard from that woman again and didn't even recall her name. He did remember her determination that if she and her family were going to make it, she had to put her total trust in God.

She had a lot in common with the two widows in today's readings. Our first reading and the Gospel tell about two poor widows who were moved to give to God all that they had — everything. We can learn a lot from them about sacrificial giving — giving back to God even if it hurts. But that isn't the only message in their stories. Their stories are also about trust — absolute, unshakable, total trust in God. When the widow in our first reading — in the midst of a terrible famine — used the last of her flour and oil to feed the prophet Elijah, she trusted in his promise that God would supply all her needs. In the Gospel story, Jesus watched another poor widow drop her last two coins into the temple treasury. Left with nothing to live on, she trusted that somehow God would take care of her. Two unnamed women — a couple of poor nobodies — teach us one of the most radical lessons from Scripture. That we should place our lives completely in God's hands and put our trust totally in God, rather than in our own human resources.

These two widows and the woman in Gary, Indiana did what would be extremely difficult for any of us. No matter how great our faith — and I know many of you have a stronger faith than I have — most of us aren't very good at putting our trust in God especially when trouble strikes. Something in us — our pride, our pigheadedness — keeps us from admitting that God is wiser than we are, that God understands things a little better than we do. We think we should be able to solve all problems, conquer all obstacles ourselves. We forget that the One who holds together all of the galaxies of the universe can certainly handle the circumstances of our puny little lives.

Trusting in God is hard because it means we have to rely on what we can't see rather than on what we can see. Almost all of you have a dollar bill in your wallet or purse. If I asked you to take it out and look at it, what would you see? What does it say? "In God We Trust." If you all waved those dollar bills in the air, what would we see? Would we see God anywhere? No, we'd see lots of money. Even though the message on the bills reminds us to trust God and not money, for many of us, it's easier to believe that cold, hard cash that we can see and feel will heal our troubles better than an unseen God.

Trusting God is hard because it requires total commitment. There's a verse from the Book of Proverbs that says, "Trust in the Lord with all your heart ...and He will make straight your paths." (Proverbs 3:3). With all your heart. That's not easy. It means there can be no half-hearted commitment. Trusting God is a lot like bunjee jumping. That's where people attach themselves to an elastic cord and jump off a bridge or a cliff. I don't know anyone who does this, but my guess is that there are no half-hearted bunjee jumpers. They must have some element of healthy fear, but they overcome it because they trust the cord enough to literally commit their life to it. Trusting God is like bunjee jumping: total, wholehearted commitment. There's a point where we decide, in spite of our fears, to jump and trust that God — our bunjee cord — won't let us crash at the bottom. And this doesn't happen just once. God asks us to jump in faith over and over again at different times in our life.

Many of us here witnessed an example of this that weekend in 2001 when our Fr. Ed Golden stood at this pulpit and courageously told us of his difficult decision to resign as pastor of the Church of the Assumption. He admitted that he was doing it with some fear and trepidation about what lay ahead, but he assured us that he made his decision with complete trust that God would lead him where he needed to be, both for his own well-being and the well-being of the Church he so faithfully serves. So, when Fr. Ed took the jump, holding tightly to his bunjee cord — what a great image — when he took that courageous leap, we knew that even in our sadness, even in our anxiety and uncertainty about Assumption's future, we too could put our trust in God, trust that God would give us what we needed to carry on without our beloved pastor,...and He did.

One final thought about trusting God. It doesn't mean we just sit back and say, "OK, Lord, you take over. I can't handle this. You do it all." That's not how God works. Here's that verse from Proverbs again: "Trust in the Lord with all your heart... and He will make straight your paths." Trust Him, and He will direct us, lead us where we need to go. Trust Him by being open to the power of His Spirit guiding and prodding and encouraging us as we pray, as we receive the Sacraments, as we meditate on Scripture, as we listen to the people He sends to us. We still have to do the hard work of living our life, facing the challenges, making the tough decisions, but we do it knowing that He is in control.

Here's a good way for you to think of it. Life is like a bike ride, but not on a regular bike, on a tandem bike — a bicycle built for two. And the two are you and Jesus. If you place your trust in Jesus, you will let Him take the front seat so that He has control of where the bike will go, while you're in the back to help Him pedal. As long as the road of your life is straight and smooth, you can relax and enjoy the ride; you don't have to pedal very hard to keep the bike moving. But when the road gets rough and rocky, when there are sharp corners to negotiate or steep hills to climb, you might become worried or anxious or afraid and it's all you can do to hang on. "Jesus, where are you taking me? I'm scared!" He'll laugh and say, "Don't worry; just keep on pedaling."

We need to be more like the two widows and the woman in Gary, Indiana and Fr. Ed Golden. We need to learn how to let Jesus steer us over and through all the obstacles, all the hazards. We need to learn to shut up and just keep on pedaling. AMEN.

CONNECTING TO THE WORD

1. Do you trust Christ, your faith, the Church? If you do, how did that trust evolve? Did a specific event secure your trust?

2. Why does our dollar bill say, "In God We Trust?" Do we trust in money or God? Are we more apt to take financial or spiritual risks?

3. When the woman in Indiana and the widows gave their resources away, where did they put their trust? Were they being reckless? Could you see yourself ever taking such a risk?

4. Identify some areas of your life that you are reluctant to turn over to God. Are you the kind of person who needs to be in charge? Would you consider it a sign of weakness to place your trust in God rather than in yourself ?

5. Has your life ever felt like you were on a solo bicycle ride? If so, what was the experience like? Have you ever pedaled in tandem with Jesus? What was that like? Which bicycle ride would you recommend to a friend?

YEAR C

THIRD SUNDAY OF ADVENT - YEAR C

Zephaniah 3:14-18; Philippians 4:4-7;
Luke 3:10-18

Rejoice! Rejoice! Rejoice!

Many of the things that make us laugh are things that weren't meant to be funny. We call them "bloopers." We all make our share of bloopers. Even church bulletins have their share of bloopers. Here are a few classics taken from actual church bulletins:

- *Attention ladies: next Saturday's rummage sale is a chance to get rid of those things not worth keeping around the house. Don't forget your husbands.*

- *The sermon at tonight's worship service will address the topic "What is Hell?" Come early and listen to our choir practice.*

- *Next Sunday is our pancake breakfast in the church hall. Fr. Mike would appreciate it if ladies of the parish would lend him their girdles.*

Here's my favorite:

- *Our men's weight-watchers group meets this Tuesday at 7PM in the church hall. Please enter through the double doors.*

You just can't make up this stuff.

I thought it would be good for us to laugh a little because the third Sunday of Advent is traditionally called *Gaudeté* Sunday; that's Latin for "Rejoice" Sunday. On Rejoice Sunday, we light the rose-colored candle on the Advent wreath, and our readings remind us of the basic mystery of our faith that even as we prepare for the Lord's coming, we have great reason to rejoice because the Lord is already here with us. Listen again to the words of the prophet Zephaniah in our first reading: "Shout for joy...The Lord your God is in your midst," and St. Paul in the second reading: "Rejoice in the Lord always! I say it again — rejoice. The Lord himself is near." And we echoed their words in our psalm response: "Cry out with joy and gladness; for among you is the Great and Holy one of Israel."

Yes, Christ is here and alive among us, here in this church and wherever two or more of us gather to pray. He is here and alive speaking to us through Sacred Scripture. He is alive in the poor, the weak, and the needy among us. He is here alive on this altar in the transformed bread and wine. He is alive inside us when we receive Him into our very own bodies. Christ is here with us - here within us. On Rejoice

Sunday, we have every reason to laugh, to rejoice and to sing for joy.

Yet, I'm sure there are some here who find this call to rejoice something of a challenge: "My husband just told me he wants a divorce. What have I got to rejoice about?"... "The biopsy report came back positive and I'm supposed to be joyful."... "I've been out of work nearly a year; our savings are almost dried up; I may have to take a job at Burger King. Rejoice? You gotta be joking."..."My mother has Alzheimers and my teenager says she hates me. You won't hear me singing for joy."

OK, so a lot of us would find it easier to be joyful if things were going a little better for us right now. And it sure would help if we didn't live in a world where so much is going wrong. When's the last time you picked up a newspaper or watched the TV news and came away with a more joyful spirit?... If it seems as if the Church's call to joy is out of synch with what's happening in our lives and in the world, maybe it's because we tend to equate "joy" with "happiness." They are not the same; they spring from two different sources. My happiness comes from what's happening to me and the world around me. Joy comes from my relationship with Christ... Happiness depends on circumstances. If things are going well in my life, if I have good health, a decent job, a good family, lots of toys and possessions, then I'm happy. But we all know that happiness can change quickly. I might wake up one morning happy as a pig in mud, but then things happen, problems arise, that dreaded phone call comes, and by the end of the day I'm anything but happy.

My joy, on the other hand, doesn't depend on external circumstances. Joy comes from inside... It comes from believing deep in my soul that Christ is constantly in my life. Joy comes from believing Jesus when He said that no matter what is happening in my life — good, bad, or in between — He will be there right smack in the center of it. It's this Christ-centered joy that can help us weather the storms when things don't go as we planned — when our wallet is almost empty, when our young people are being shipped off to war, when our family is in turmoil, in the intensive-care waiting room, when things can't get any worse.

Zephaniah and Paul understood this. They didn't write the words we just heard while they were on a tropical beach sipping piña coladas. Zephaniah was writing during the anguish and distress of the Jewish exile, when the people were captive in a foreign land. Paul was writing from a prison cell, isolated from those he loved and longed for. Yet neither of them would let their desperate circumstances rob them of joy because their joy sprang from their deep belief that no matter how bad things got, God was close at hand. God would give them the strength to endure. God would eventually make things better, set things right. So they could say to their people, "Don't be discouraged; don't be anxious. Things don't look so good right now, but rejoice, the Lord is with us. "...This message is also meant for all of us to hear today.

My friends, we need to realize that there are a lot of circumstances we can't control, but we can control our response to them. Whether a difficult circumstance defeats us or strengthens us depends on how we respond to it. Our natural response is to feel sorry for ourselves, to wonder, "Why me?" Our natural response is to become anxious and fearful. Our natural response is to worry about what is going to happen next. Someone said, "worry" is like a rocking chair. It gives you something to do, but it doesn't get you anywhere. But we can choose to respond unnaturally. We can choose joy. We can choose to trust the hand of our Living God even when we don't understand what's going on. We can choose to believe that God is indeed working for the good... even though we can't see how. It won't remove the pain, but it will enable us to live joyfully in spite of it.

Now, by living joyfully I don't mean we should go skipping and giggling through the day like Pollyanna, ignoring the harsh realities of life. I mean that this Christ-centered joy enables us to more readily find joy in those ordinary things that are all around us: the smile on a child's face; the touch of a loved one's hand; the bright sun on a crisp winter day; a phone call from a friend; a Christmas tree all decorated and twinkling; the smell of turkey roasting in the oven. Ordinary things, ordinary events, ordinary people, yet not so ordinary, because each is a gift from the One who is the source of all our joy.

This then, is the message we need to remember as we move through Advent toward the joy of Christmas day: that we have great reason to rejoice

RIGHT NOW, for the Lord our God is here with us. Our Lord loves us in spite of all of our flaws and weaknesses. Our Lord forgives us and lifts us up when we fall. Our Lord wants our hearts to be filled with joy, not because we're free of trouble and tears, but because we're free of any fear that we are alone. Our Lord feeds and strengthens us as He will in a few moments with His Precious Body and Blood. Our Lord — for reasons we can never understand — wants you and me to spend eternity with Him, so much so that He willingly went to the cross so that the doorway to Heaven would be open to us. (I hope it's a double door so we'll have no trouble getting in)… My friends, what more could we ask for? What more reasons do we need to rejoice? AMEN!.

CONNECTING TO THE WORD

1. Think of the times of sadness, stress, and sorrow in your life. Did your faith help you find peace in the middle of these storms? Did you give faith a chance to be an anchor in your stormy life? If so, did you rejoice or offer thanks after the turbulence calmed?

2. At the height of a crisis, have you known a greater sense of gratitude for the blessings in your life? If so, how did you rejoice?

3. Have you ever exchanged pleasure for joy in your life? If so, why? Do you know joy today? If so, describe it. If not, simply reflect on experiences that have brought a smile to your face in the past.

4. Which things in your life would cause you to shout out for joy like Paul and Zephaniah? If you shouted out a joyful message, how do you think those near and dear to you would respond?

5. Where is Christ near in your life? Make a list and after each instance rejoice privately and think of a way you can rejoice publicly as well.

SECOND SUNDAY OF LENT – YEAR C

Luke 9:28-36

Listen To Him!

In today's Gospel, Peter, James and John witness the amazing Transfiguration of Jesus. Before their very eyes, the face of Jesus becomes as radiant as the sun, His clothes like dazzling white light. The three disciples get a glimpse of the true Christ in all His heavenly glory — the glory He would return to only after He had endured the suffering and death that loomed ahead in Jerusalem. Peter is awestruck by the scene of the transfigured Jesus talking with the great prophets Moses and Elijah, and He tells Jesus he wants to erect a tent for each of them. But before he gets the words out of his mouth, the whole scene is overshadowed by a great cloud from which the voice of God speaks: "This is my chosen Son.... Listen to Him!"...Listen to Him.

Hearing these words from out of the cloud, those three disciples shed any doubts they might have had about who this Jesus was, and whether He truly spoke for God. He alone must be listened to. And that is what God commands each of us to do — LISTEN TO HIM! Because when Jesus speaks, it is God speaking. It is God telling us how we can get to where He wants us to be, how we can grow into a mature, complete Christian. So God commands us, "Listen to Him!"

But that's hard to do today. We live in a world that is filled with more voices than ever before. You don't like what's on TV — change the channel. Cable has hundreds of stations. If you don't like any of those, you can rent from thousands of videos or DVDs. Or you can surf thousands of websites. While you're driving, you have every kind of radio station to occupy your mind, or countless CDs to play. Then you have all those competing voices at home — the kids, the spouse, the parents, neighbors, friends — and of course the ones at work or at school. All of them demanding so much of our attention that it's almost impossible to even hear Jesus let alone listen to Him.

We have to work hard to stay "tuned in" to Jesus, to what He tells us is best for us. And we have to "tune out" the opposing voices, the ones tempting us to go with our feelings and our passions, without regard to any standards of right and wrong. The ones telling us, "If it feels right for you, then go ahead — do it... How can it be wrong if it feels so right?" With this approach to life, how we feel is more important than what Jesus says. But if we are going to listen to Jesus, feelings and passions are OK, we just can't let them ever overrule what Jesus is calling us to do. Jesus never tells us how we should feel. He tells us how we should be, how we should act. It's what we do that matters, not how we feel. If we listen to Him,

He doesn't say, "Go with your gut, go with your feelings." He says, "Do what is right."

Many people do try to listen to Jesus and live by His teachings, but they still mess up their lives. They're like the backwoods farmer who bought a chain saw because the hardware clerk told him he could cut down a lot more trees in a lot less time. This poor fellow had never seen a chain saw before, but he took it to try it out. He came back the next day and demanded his money back saying, "This saw didn't help me at all. I used it all day and I only cut down one lousy tree." The clerk didn't understand how that could be. He took the saw from the farmer, looked it over, then pulled the cord. When the chain saw roared to life, the backwoods farmer jumped back and cried, "What's that noise?!" The poor guy had taken this new kind of saw and had used it the old way.[1]

Some of us do the same thing. We want to listen to Jesus and follow Jesus, but we're stuck in the old way we've lived for so long. We can't seem to shake loose from the world's hold on us and give ourselves totally to Christ. In John 17:14 Jesus says of His followers, "They do not belong to the world." He doesn't want to share us with the world. He wants all of us. A man once said to another man, "All you Christians are brainwashed." The Christian man replied, "Everybody's brainwashed. But we've chosen who we want to wash our brains — Jesus Christ."

Now there are people who say, if we listen to Jesus (let Him brainwash us), then it's like, "Don't do this. Don't do that. Don't act that way; act this way. We have no freedom. We're stuck living by all these rules. I want to be free to do whatever I want, free to enjoy life." Friends, they are so wrong. It's exactly the opposite. In John 8:31-32, Jesus says, "If you live in my word,... you will know the truth, and the truth will set you free." Listening to Jesus doesn't make me a slave; it makes me free. Not free to do whatever I want to do. That's not freedom; that's opening the door to a new kind of slavery. A cheating spouse says "I want to be free to play around even though I'm married.".... A drug dealer says, "I want to be free to sell drugs whenever I want and to whomever I want.".... A greedy businessperson says, "I want to be free to make as much money as I can, any way I can.".... That's not freedom; that's being a slave to Satan, a slave to all those ways and those things that Satan keeps trying to convince the world are OK.

When I listen to Jesus, it frees me from the pressure to conform to the world's ways, from having to be what the world says I should be. I'm free to become everything God created me to be. I don't have to be something I was never supposed to be. Let me give an example. Suppose I was a fish, and I spent day after day at the bottom of the ocean, year after year in the water, and I'm getting sick of it. I wanna get free of the water and go on dry land where I can roam with the lions and the tigers and all the other animals. I wanna get free of this water and get to do what I want to do. So one day I start swimming close to the shore and I let the tide wash me up onto the beach. Finally, I'm free from the water and I'm on land right where I wanna be and I cry out, "Free at last, free at last. Thank God Almighty, I'm free at last!" But then it dawns on me: I can't breathe. I can't survive on land... "Fool at last! Fool at last!" Because I'm not free if I'm a fish on dry land. God created me to swim in water, not walk on land. And as soon as I try to be other than what God created me to be, I'm not free — I'm dead![2]

So when we listen to Jesus, and He tells us, "Don't do that, do this. Don't act that way, act this way," He's not trying to make life tough for you and me. He's not trying to take the fun out of our life. He's setting us free — free to be the wonderful people God created us to be — so that you and I may live and not die — ever. We may live forever. AMEN.

CONNECTING TO THE WORD

1. Do you think Christ appeared in dazzling white light because he was transformed, or was it the spiritual insight of the disciples that was transformed? Or had God trusted them enough to allow them to see His Son's always existent, true self?

2. Reflect on the pros and cons of Christ's non-conformity. Do the benefits outweigh the drawbacks? What situations in your life call for conformity? What situations call for non-conformity? Are there any situations in which you would rather not conform?

3. Do you only engage in activities that make you feel good? Do you consult Christ or your faith community before making major decisions? If you are happy but others are not happy, do you feel left out? What resources does your faith offer you that can assist in making decisions that are faith driven rather than group-think driven?

4. Is it possible that when your relationship with Christ is in jeopardy so is your relationship with yourself and others? How can you keep your relationship with Christ new? Does your peer group encourage spiritual growth and commitment? Do your peers allow you to articulate this aspect of your life freely? Have others tried to

dissuade you from your Christian roots? Did they succeed? Have you recovered your lost beliefs?

5. In public, do you present yourself as Christ made you to be or do you present yourself in a way that is pleasing to others rather than to yourself or Christ?

NOTES

1. This story adapted from Tony Evans, *The Perfect Christian* (Nashville: Word Publishing, 1998), 128
2. Adapted from *Commitment to Truth,* a tape series by Dr. Anthony Evans (Dallas: The Urban Alternative, 2000)

SECOND SUNDAY OF ORDINARY TIME - YEAR C

*Isaiah 15; 1Corinthians 12:4-11; **John 2:1-12***

When The Wine Runs Out

In case you haven't guessed it from my name, I am Italian. In fact, my ethnic heritage is one hundred percent Italian, so I feel well qualified to make the following statement. *There is no way that today's Gospel story would've happened if Jesus had been born and lived his life in Italy.* You see, there has never been, and there never will be, an Italian wedding where they run out of anything — and certainly not wine. Any self-respecting Italian family — rich or poor — would rather go into debt than have people saying behind their backs, "Remember the day they ran out of wine at so and so's wedding?"

Well, fortunately, Jesus was born a Jew, not an Italian, so we do have this wonderful Gospel story in which He performs the first of His miracles at a wedding feast in Cana. After a little gentle persuasion from His mother (after all, that's what mothers do best, and from what I've seen and heard, Jewish mothers do it especially well) Jesus saves the bride and groom from an embarrassment that could've ruined what should be the happiest day of their lives. The miracle Jesus performs at their wedding was the first sign of who Jesus was — the long-awaited Messiah, promised by God. His changing of water into wine was the first sign that God's power was truly at work in Jesus.

Now, there are a lot of symbols and layers of meaning in this story — as there are throughout John's Gospel. But I want to focus on those words that Mary utters right at the beginning: "They have no more wine." These words not only lead to the miracle of Jesus transforming ordinary water into superb new wine, these words also speak about so many of us today whose lives are in need of Jesus' transforming power. Lives in which *the wine has run out.* I've heard it, and you've heard it repeated many, many times, expressed in different ways: "The honeymoon is over."... "Things just aren't like they used to be."... "My life's going nowhere."... "It's no use, I'm tired, I give up." Or words like these. Words that reveal an emptiness, a sense that something has gone out of our lives, that our lives are flat and meaningless, our faith seems dull and lifeless, and we are past the point of hoping that it can change. *Our wine has run out.*

We've all been there. Some of us are there right now. It could be that after a few years or quite a few years of marriage, your dreams have gone, your love has stopped growing, and you've settled into a humdrum routine. *Your wine has run out...* It could be that your faith was vibrant and alive when things were going well, but when someone you loved so much died, your faith died with them and it's all you can do to just keep going. *Your wine has run out...* It could be that your family life has been growing more and more tense, and after that last big blowup, nothing you do seems to help; nothing seems to make any difference. *Your wine has run out.*

It could be that your work used to be so stimulating and fulfilling that you couldn't wait to get there every morning. Now it's like being on death row, waiting to see who they will come for next... It could be that it was easy for you to talk about hope when it was someone else who was in despair, but when you found out you had a terrible sickness, *the wine of hope had ran out...*Or maybe you're feeling old. You're worn out and weary, and you find yourself thinking more and more, "It doesn't matter anymore; my life is over." *Your wine has run out.*

It is at these points in our lives that today's Gospel comes along and says: this is where Christ enters, and He not only enters, but He enters with the power to transform — the power to touch the ordinary water of our lives and change it into new wine, new hope, new beginnings. Not in the Pollyanna sense that everything will be wonderful and perfect, and we will go smiling and tip-toeing through the tulips, but in the sense that no matter how deeply mired we are in pain or doubts or despair, He can make growth and fulfillment come out of it.

Today's Gospel ask us to believe that Jesus Christ will come and transform your life and mine, make all things new again. So we must ask ourselves, "Do we really believe this? Or is it just more pious preaching? It would be nice if it happened, but do we really believe it?" ... I believe it because I've seen it happen, time and again, most recently to a young family whose rebellious son fled from their good, Christian home, rejecting all of their values, to take up a life of drugs and Satanism and a punk-rocker lifestyle. This was a family that for three years tried everything they could to get their son back. This was a family that was on the edge of giving up hope they would ever be a complete family again. *Their wine had almost run out...* Then they decided to entrust their son to the Lord's care, to open their hearts to the hope in His power to transform lives. I saw the fruits of that trust and hope the last time I dropped in on them — unvited. As I walked into their kitchen, I almost fell over when right there before my eyes, seated at the table, was their prodigal son, looking and talking like any normal nineteen-year-old, diligently filling out college applications. When his mother saw the look of surprise on my face, she smiled and said, "Our prayers have been answered."

Tomorrow we celebrate the birthday of another man who believed in Christ's power to transform hearts, to transform people. The Reverend Martin Luther King never moaned about the fact that the wine of freedom was drying up in America. He believed deeply in the power of God's grace not only to change water into wine, but to change hearts of stone into hearts of flesh. His dream of making our great nation even greater and more just, wakened us to begin to change.

Christ burst into a world that desperately needed to change. He came to change things, to change people — just as he changed water into wine. A few weeks ago as we welcomed the New Year, many of us made the same old familiar resolutions to be better people and change how we live. If we really want to change our lives, we need to follow those other words Mary spoke at the wedding, "Do whatever he tells you."... We have to listen to her son's voice as He speaks to us in Scripture, in our prayer, in the circumstances and people of our lives, and then, like the servants at the wedding, we have to do what He says. When we do that, we can be certain He will not let us run out of wine; He will change the ordinary water of our lives into superb new wine — a wine of love and peace and joy that will flow... forever. AMEN.

CONNECTING TO THE WORD

1. During the wedding at Cana, Jesus gave the first glimpse into His divinity. If you had been at the wedding would you have believed Him if He simply introduced himself as the Messiah?

2. Have you encountered signs of Jesus' ability to work miracles in your life today? If so, have these signs re-affirmed a faith that was always inside of you? Do you need dramatic miracles to keep your faith alive ? What are some of the little, everyday miracles that help to sustain your faith in Christ?

3. Did Christ perform the miracle at Cana to get the attention of others, or did H do it to offer His Father's children an example of transformation? When you have performed a Christian act of kindness, what was your motivation for doing so?

4. Has the wine run out in one or more areas of your life? If it has, has anyone come to offer assistance? Have you ever come to another person's aid when he or she was out of wine?

5. Martin Luther King Jr. was an articulate child of God. He delivered and lived Christ's message in his everyday life and in his fight for social justice. How did his actions, and the actions of those like him, plant the seeds of miracles in our lives?

FOURTH SUNDAY OF ORDINARY TIME - YEAR C

Jeremiah 1:4-5,17-19; 1Corinthians 12:31 – 13:13;
Luke 4:21-30

Handling The Truth [1]

We just heard St. Luke's account of what happened the first time Jesus preached in His hometown of Nazareth in front of the people who had watched Him grow up. According to Luke, that homily produced quite a reaction... I remember the first time I preached in my hometown. Luckily, I didn't get the kind of response Jesus got. Nobody tried to run me out of town and throw me off a cliff. Yet I can imagine that as I was speaking from the pulpit, some of the congregation were thinking things like: "Isn't this Joe the barber's son?... Isn't this the same little Ronnie who used to run down the street with his diaper falling down around his knees?... Where did he learn all this stuff he's telling us?... Boy, God sure has a strange sense of humor." They may have been thinking that, but when it was over they patted me on the back and told me they were proud of me. It was nothing like the reaction Jesus got. That's because I had preached the Good News; I had told them what they wanted to hear.

That day in the synagogue, Jesus had started out telling the people what they wanted to hear. After reading the prophecy from Isaiah, Jesus announced that He was the fulfillment of that prophecy — the long awaited Messiah who would bring Good News to the poor, proclaim liberty to captives, give sight to the blind, and set free the oppressed. When they heard this, Luke says, the people "spoke highly of Him and were amazed at the gracious words that came from His mouth." But then, moments later, they turned on Him. What had Jesus done that changed them from an admiring throng into an angry mob that wanted to kill him?... He had told them the truth.

He reminded them of two Old Testament episodes in which God's prophets had ministered to "foreigners" — people whom Israel looked upon as their enemies. This was Jesus' way of explaining to them that God's love is universal – it's for all the children of His creation not just a chosen few. Hearing Him speak this way, the synagogue crowd was outraged. Jesus was a threat to their expectation that God would send them a Messiah King who would lead them to victory over their enemies, not minister to them. They threw Jesus out of the synagogue because they couldn't stand to hear the truth.

There was a movie some years back called *A Few Good Men*. In it there was a powerful scene where a young military lawyer played by Tom Cruise is interrogating a crusty general played by Jack Nicholson. The lawyer confronts the general on the accuracy of his testimony, looks him in the eyes and says, "Sir, tell us the truth."... And with a sneering expression that is vintage Jack Nicholson, the general responds, "Truth? You can't handle the truth!"... That day in the synagogue the people of Nazareth couldn't handle the truth... This raises the question, "How are we at handling the truth, the truth given to us by Jesus Christ, the Son of God, who is the way and the TRUTH and the life?"... Do we accept and embrace His words and commit ourselves to live by them? Or is His truth too much for us to handle? Do we like the world's version of the truth better? Is it easier to accept, easier to handle?

St. Paul, in one of his farewell speeches in the Book of Acts, warns us to be on guard against deceivers who will come among us distorting the truth (Acts 20:29-30). These deceivers are every-where: in politics and government, in our schools and universities and corporations, in our movies and music, on TV and radio, even in some churches. They tell us what we ought to think and believe and do... And they make it sound so good even though it's totally counter to the teaching of Jesus Christ.

We can easily get sucked in by their version of the truth, because a lot of the truth from Jesus isn't designed to make us FEEL good; it's designed to make us DO good. Sure, some of what He tells us makes us feel good. In almost every church on every weekend, you will hear about God's mercy and forgiveness, about God's unconditional love for us, about the promise of eternal life, how Christ understands our suffering, how He comes to us in the Eucharist...We need to hear these things to inspire and encourage us to deal with the harsh realities of life. But church isn't a place we come to week after week simply to have our ears tickled, simply to feel good. It should be a place where we are confronted with the WHOLE truth of Jesus Christ — truth that cuts both ways.

If you leave here happy every Sunday, something is wrong. If you leave here doing spiritual somersaults every week, something is wrong. Every now and then you should leave here crying, weeping, uncomfortable, maybe even angry because you heard the truth of Jesus Christ that challenged you to be better than you are, truth that would make you stop doing some of the things you've been doing and stop thinking some of the things you've been thinking. That should happen here in church too.

It doesn't happen very often. We preachers want everyone to like us. We don't want to offend anybody. We'd rather preach a sermon that says, "I'm OK, you're OK, God loves us just the way we are." That's less risky than a sermon that reminds us of the things in our lives and in the world that are wrong, that need to be changed if we truly want to follow Christ. How often do you hear from a pulpit: abortion is wrong; cheating on your wife or husband is wrong; beating up on your spouse is wrong; sex outside of marriage is wrong; the death penalty is wrong; abusing drugs or alcohol is wrong; prejudice and bigotry are wrong; an economic system that makes the rich richer and the poor poorer is wrong?

Maybe it's because this kind of truth is so hard for people to handle. Maybe we preachers worry about the congregation turning on us as they did on Jesus at Nazareth. I don't know, but we really need to hear the WHOLE truth of Jesus Christ — not just what makes us feel good. We need to hear it, embrace it, and commit ourselves to live it. We need to follow the One who speaks the truth, whose life testified to the truth, and not be deceived by the lies the world feeds to us as truth.

There were two farmers, Pete and Jake, who every year would bet each other that their best horse could beat the other's best horse in a race. And every year, Pete's horse would win the race. Jake was tired of losing, so he decided to secretly hire a professional jockey to ride his horse and give him the winning edge. The race began and the two black stallions were running side by side with the professional jockey keeping Jake's horse barely in front. They stayed that way until at the turn into the home stretch the horses collided and horses and riders all fell to the ground. As they laid there, farmer Jake's jockey, who had a lot of experience with this sort of thing, jumped right up, got on the horse and crossed the finish line, the crowd cheering him on. Jake had finally won. But wait a minute.There was Jake upset, shaking his head, going crazy. Someone said "What's wrong? Your man got over the finish line first. Why are you upset?" Jake looked at him and said, "'Cause he got on the wrong horse!"

My friends, watch what horse you're riding. Ride on King Jesus, because if you ride on the wrong horse, you may get to the finish line thinking you made it... but you will have lost the race. Jesus Christ is the truth! AMEN.

CONNECTING TO THE WORD

1. Have you ever severed a relationship with someone because he or she spoke the truth to you? If so, was it done lovingly or with malice? Was he or she delivering his or her version of the truth or was he or she offering a truth that could cut and free you from personal denial?

2. Have you severed yourself from Christ because you weren't ready to hear His truth? Or have you heard his truth and interpreted it to suit your own needs? Has Christ ever intervened in your life through circumstances, events, or people to help you hear and adhere to His truth?

3. Is your parish honest about both its strengths and its shortcomings? Does your faith community and the Catholic church at large, adhere to Christ's message? If so, how is this accomplished? If not, what could you do to bring your community and the Catholic church at large to the forefront of its failings so that it can best uphold and support its doctrine and God's people?

4. Reflect on one truth in your life with which you have recently come to terms. Did this acceptance give you freedom? Did it improve your relationship with yourself, with Christ, to those near and dear to you, and with your faith community as well?

NOTES

1. The stories and some ideas used in this homily are adapted from a set of tapes entitled *Commitment to Truth* by Dr. Anthony T. Evans, produced and distributed by The Urban Alternative, Dallas, Texas.

EIGHTH SUNDAY OF ORDINARY TIME - YEAR C

Sirach 27:4-7; 1Corinthians 15:54-58;
Luke 6:39-45

Jesus The Heart Doctor

One of my all-time favorite sports personalities was Casey Stengel, long time baseball manager who had a colorful way with the English language. It was called "Stengelese." After he retired from baseball, Casey took a position on the board of directors of a large California bank. It was kind of a strange job for a gruff, old baseball man, so a reporter once asked Casey to describe his duties. He responded in typical Stengelese: "Son, there ain't nothin' to it. You go into this fancy meeting room and you sit there and you never open your yap. As long as you don't say nuthin', they don't know whether your smart or dumb." Pretty good advice, but I don't know too many of us who follow it. In fact, according to statisticians, the average man speaks about 25,000 words a day; the average woman, 30,000. Each of us engages in about thirty conversations every day. So there's plenty of opportunity for people to gauge how smart or how dumb we are.

But that's not all that our words reveal about us. In our first reading, Sirach uses everyday images to make the point that what a person says tells us a lot about them: "The fruit of a tree shows the care it has had; so too does a man's speech disclose the bent of his mind." In the Gospel, Jesus takes this tree/fruit image a bit further when He says, "A good tree does not bear rotten fruit, nor does a rotten tree bear good fruit... A good person out of the store of goodness in his heart produces good, but an evil person out of a store of evil produces evil, for from the fullness of the heart the mouth speaks." Both of these are saying: listen to a person talk, and you will eventually learn what that person is, his or her true nature. The words we speak are a window into our heart, our character.

There are two important messages we can draw from this today. Number one: **words have power**. Words matter a lot. We sometimes forget this. We often say that "talk is cheap" and "what we do is more important than what we say." But if we're spewing out 25 to 30 thousand words a day, we can be sure that some of them will have a strong impact on other people. We are reminded of this in other parts of the Bible. For example, In James 3:1-10, the writer tells us that even though the tongue is a small part of our body, it is a very powerful part, able to do both great good and great evil. And Sirach 28:18 tells us that many more have fallen by the tongue than have fallen by the sword. Our words do have the power to impact others.

There's a true story that's been making the rounds on the Internet about a busy executive who

had just been told by his co-workers how appreciated he was. As he drove home that night feeling so
good about hearing this, he realized that lately he had
been coming down pretty hard on his 14-year old son
and he hadn't let him know how much he loved and
appreciated him... That night he told him. The boy
broke down crying, and through his tears he said to
his father, "Dad, today I wrote a letter to you and
Mom telling you I was sorry for killing myself and
asking for your forgiveness. I was going to commit
suicide tonight; I didn't think you cared about me at
all. But after what you just told me, I can tear up the
letter." Our words do have power.

Christian writer Max Lucado tells about a courageous woman he knew who had waged a very tough
battle against alcoholism, and was doing all she
could to restore her relationship with God. She chose
a small church to attend where she knew many of the
members, hoping that she would be accepted there.
One Sunday as she walked from her car to the church,
she overheard two women nearby. Their stinging
words weren't meant for her to hear, but she heard
them anyway: "How long is that alcoholic going to
hang around here?" The woman turned and walked
back to her car. She never entered another church
building again...until she died[1]. Words have power.

Since words have so much power, we have to ask
ourselves: How do my words impact others? Do my
words lift others up or do they tear them down? Do my
words calm, soothe, heal, and encourage or do they
wound and berate? Is my normal mode of conversation one of complaining, criticizing, nitpicking?

Am I quick to point out the speck in someone else's eye but miss the plank in my own? Do I use words to label people, attack them, slander them? Are my words loaded with prejudice against those who are different? Do I use words to belittle or degrade others so that I look good, so that I can feel superior? Or do I say what makes others feel better and look good ?

After we honestly answer these questions, we come to the second important message from today's readings: **the words we speak reflect our character**. Words don't just pop out of thin air. Jesus says they come from the heart, revealing the type of person we are on the inside, just as the quality of a tree's fruit tells us what the tree is like on the inside. What this means is that if the wrong kind of words keep coming from our mouth, then there is something wrong on the inside; we have a heart problem that is worse than a clogged artery or an erratic heartbeat. Our heart hasn't allowed the transforming power of God's Spirit to do its thing — to make it more like the heart of Jesus. We may call ourselves Christians; we may call ourselves believers. But if we are locking His Spirit out, keeping Him from transforming our heart, our words, our actions, then we haven't truly put our faith in Jesus Christ, because we haven't let Him take over our heart.

There are some of us who suffer from this heart problem most of the time; we have chronic heart disease. The rest of us exhibit symptoms only now and then. But we all need the help of the heart specialist — Jesus Christ. And there's no better time to make an appointment with Him than during the season of Lent that starts on Wednesday — a season for reflection and renewal and healing. A time to go to Him and ask Him to cure any sickness in our heart that comes out in the words we speak. Ask Him to cure all of the fears, all the insecurities, all of the unhealthy attitudes that shape the words we use. Ask Him to mold our heart to be more like His. Let's make that our Lenten mission.

My friends, if I huff and puff as I walk up the stairs, if sharp pains are shooting across my chest, if my pulse is irregular, there is probably something seriously wrong with my physical heart — the organ that pumps my blood. I would be a fool if I didn't go to the doctor to check it out. If the wrong kind of words come out of my mouth, if the things I say don't sound anything like what Jesus would say, it's a sign that there is something wrong with my spiritual heart — the core of who I am. I would be a fool if I didn't go to the Lord to check it out. Whether it's our physical heart or our spiritual heart, I don't think anyone of us can afford to be a fool. AMEN.

CONNECTING TO THE WORD

1. Try to visualize if the words you attach to your thoughts and feelings stem from a healthy branch that offers healthy fruit or from an unhealthy branch that would offer rotten fruit.

2. Has anyone ever spoken to you in a manner that has stymied your growth process? Has anyone ever spoken to you in a manner that has encouraged your personal growth? What is your communication style? Is it growth-reductive or growth-supportive?

3. Does your church community welcome each tree, healthy or unhealthy, into its forest? Has your church leadership encouraged you to tend God's soil with care and with love? Have you ever heard harsh, unwelcoming words spoken in your place of worship? If so, how did you respond?

4. When you criticize an individual or group, is it done constructively to earnestly help them or is it done to cut them down so that you or like-minded people appear taller? Is your heart clogged with words of hate and harsh criticism or is it flowing with words of acceptance and love?

NOTES

1. This story was taken from Max Lucado's *On the Anvil* (New York: Walker and Company, 1996), 167.

Luke 13:22-30

Leave That Backpack Behind

A priest had just given a very inspiring sermon about the afterlife. When he was finished, he said to the congregation: "Stand up if you think you're going to heaven." Everyone in the church stood up. When they sat back down, he said: "Stand up if you think you're going to hell." No one stood up except one man way in the back of the church. The priest asked him: "You really think you're going to hell?" The man replied, "Uh,… well, no, Father, but I hated to see you standing there alone."

Several recent polls showed that 80-90% of Americans expect to go to heaven. Is that expectation realistic? Or are people taking heaven for granted? This issue is addressed in today's Gospel. There is no more important issue than our eternal destiny. According to the Bible — especially in the words from Jesus — every one of us will go to heaven or to hell forever. People ask me why we rarely ever preach on this topic, and I usually mumble something about having to stick to what's in the readings for the day... I guess I can't use that excuse today. To be honest, I don't preach on this topic for the same reason I don't go out of my way to have a root canal — it's not all that pleasant... My preaching professor told us over and over: "Tell them the Good News. Tell them the Good News."... How do you find Good News in a gospel passage that uses images like a narrow gate, a locked door, wailing and gnashing of teeth, and words like "I don't know where you are from. Depart from me you evildoers."?... Well, I'm going to try.

In this Gospel passage when Jesus is asked about people being saved, and He answers by talking about the "narrow gate" and a locked door, He is speaking about entrance into heaven. When Jesus says, "Strive to enter the narrow gate, for many will try to enter but will not get in," He's saying we shouldn't take heaven for granted. We have to "strive", we have to make every effort, to enter. In other words, there's something we have to do to get to heaven. Now is Jesus saying that we should make every effort to be a good person because only those who are good enough will get in? No, the whole Bible, including Jesus's teaching, makes it clear that no one can be good enough to deserve heaven. As St. Paul wrote in Romans 3:23: "All have sinned and fall short of the Glory of God."

Our salvation, our getting to heaven, is only possible as a free gift from God — pure grace — through the sacrifice of His Son... If we could be good enough, then Jesus wouldn't have had to die in our place. His suffering, death and resurrection make it possible for every person — good and not so good — to be saved, to get through that narrow gate. So, if heaven is a free gift purchased for us by the blood of Christ, then why do we need to do anything? Because, whenever we are offered any gift, it requires a response. We can accept the gift. We can refuse it. We can say, "Thank you, what a thoughtful gift," then put it away and forget about it. We can accept the gift and later decide it takes too much effort to use it (like the cappuccino maker that's gathering dust on my shelf). Or we can accept the gift and use it as the giver intended.

My friends, the God that was revealed to the world in the person of Jesus Christ is a God of love and mercy, a God who wants every one of His children to be saved, a God who wants every one of His children to get through that narrow gate. He doesn't want to hear any of us desperately knocking at that locked door. God offers each of us the undeserved gift of eternal life in His heavenly kingdom and He wants us to use that gift — that promise — to make life better right here in His earthly kingdom. And the way we do this — the way we make this life better — is to strive to be like the One who made that gift possible, strive to be like Jesus.

You see, when we say we believe in Jesus Christ as our Savior, as the one who opened the gate of heaven for us, our faith isn't authentic and complete unless we also accept everything He said and did, and unless we intend — with the grace of the Sacraments and the help of the Holy Spirit — to do our best to live the way He lived...We can't just accept Jesus as our Savior and ignore the hard stuff. It's only by living our faith that we'll get through that narrow gate into heaven...We have to be like the hiker I read about who got trapped in a cave. He found a small opening to escape, but he couldn't squeeze through it with his backpack. He had to remove the backpack and leave it behind in order to slip through the narrow opening to safety. When we come to the gate of heaven, we can't come loaded down with a backpack full of sinful habits and sinful attitudes or we won't fit through the gate... And then there's only one place left for us to go.

Which brings us to the topic most of us would rather avoid: hell. But we can't. The same Bible which teaches that God in mercy and love sent Christ to die for sinners, also teaches that our God is a God of perfect holiness and a God of justice who hates sin, and will punish those who cling to sin and refuse to repent, who reject the gift of salvation He has offered. The Bible, and especially Jesus, have spoken plainly and clearly on the subject of hell. Unless we take a scissors and cut their words out of our Bibles, we must believe that there is a place or a state of existence in which unrepentant sinners are punished... This belief in the reality of hell serves a powerful purpose... It functions kind of like the cellar in the house that I grew up in. Our cellar was dark and damp and had a big hole in one corner that my brother and I called "the sewer" because that's how it smelled. And we could swear that rats — slimy, beady-eyed rats — were swimming around in that smelly cesspool... I was terrified to be in the cellar alone. So, how do you think my dad punished me when I was bad? Down in the cellar... alone. The most terrifying words I heard growing up were "Go to the cellar."... The existence of that cellar down below had a huge impact on my behavior.

I knew that my father loved me, and most of the time, that love was enough to keep me from doing bad things. But there were times when temptation was so strong, or my spirit was so rebellious, that love wasn't enough to keep me in check, but the thought of his anger and the fear of what awaited in that cellar was usually enough to straighten me out (not always, but usually). It's like that with our heavenly Father. We know He loves us, and most of the time that love will be enough for us to follow Him. But there are times when temptation becomes so strong that it blocks out any thoughts of God's love. It's in those moments, that the Holy Spirit may nudge us and remind us of "the cellar". And the reminder that there is a place of punishment, just might convince us to correct our behavior.

Jesus gives us such a reminder in today's Gospel. The image of the locked door, people not being let in. The image of the wailing and gnashing of teeth as the condemned are on the outside looking in, watching as people from the four corners of the earth enjoy the great banquet in the heavenly kingdom...This vision of hell may not be as frightening as others in the Bible, yet it does powerfully convey the utter sense of loss and despair, the awareness of being totally rejected by God, and the realization that this is it for eternity. It won't change. It's too late.

So, where's the Good News in all this? The Good News for us is that it's not too late as long as there is breath in our bodies. In this life, God gives us chance after chance to prepare ourselves for that moment when we stand before that narrow gate. Through the Sacraments of the Church, God gives us the grace to start over every time we fall. The Holy Spirit prompts and prods us all our lives to reform and do the right thing. But in the end, my friends, it is up to us. God doesn't send us to heaven or to hell; we make that choice. He wants all of us to choose heaven... So let's choose it today. Let's not be like those who say , "I'll take care of that tomorrow; today I want to live my life my way."... Because only God knows if tomorrow will come. AMEN.

CONNECTING TO THE WORD

1. Parents create fearful consequences for their children to keep them from engaging in behavior that may hurt themselves or others. Think of actions/choices in your life right now, and decide if any of them can lead to hurtful outcomes for yourself or others. If you find that you have set out on a potentially hurtful path or are about to, how can your faith help you to alter your course of action?

2. Do you carry any hurtful views of yourself or others around with you? Do these views allow you to hear only bits and pieces of Christ´s message instead of its whole?

3. Define "sin" in your own words. If you have trouble defining it, speak to a minister in your faith community about this topic. Afterward, reflect on your conversational findings and try to determine if the backpack of sin you carry is over-stuffed with sin or filled with a realistic, limited amount of sin.

4. Think of ways that Christ´s love can help you to better manage the accumulation of sin that you carry with you through your earthly life. What aspects of Christ´s message will help you to leave it all behind?

Sirach 3:17-20, 28-29; Hebrews 12:18-19, 22-24;
Luke 14:1, 7-14

Guess Who's Coming To Dinner?

Today's Gospel Story is one of three different occasions where Jesus was invited to dine with a Pharisee and his guests. In each case Jesus proceeds to tell his host and the other guests not what they want to hear, but what they need to hear. In today's story, Jesus scolds the Pharisees for the arrogant way they jockey for positions of honor at the table, and then He finds fault with his host for inviting only "proper" people to his banquet. After reading stories like today's Gospel, we can be pretty certain that the Pharisees found that meal time with Jesus could cause a serious case of indigestion.

But Jesus' challenging words to the Pharisees are also meant for our 21st-century ears. When Jesus tells us not to invite our friends or relatives or wealthy or important individuals to dinner, but to invite instead the poor and the crippled, the weak and the outcasts, all those on the margins of society, we shouldn't be surprised. These are the ones Jesus identified with and was drawn to wherever He went. These are the ones in whom we are to recognize His presence: "Whatever you do to the least of my brothers and sisters, you do to me."

What Jesus is asking us to do is to give the poor and the lowly among us the same priority that He has given them. He wants us to extend our hospitality and generosity not only to those who are able to return our hospitality and generosity, but also to those who cannot repay us, and even to the ones who may be too proud or too ashamed to say thank you. Here Jesus is calling on Christians not only to provide for the needs of the poor and the disabled; He's telling us "invite them to dinner." He's calling on His church not to just give them food or clothes or money, He's telling us, "invite them to your church gatherings, make them welcome as equals, share fellowship with them, break bread together."

Three weeks ago, our parish enjoyed a sunny and glorious picnic celebration — an afternoon of food, fun, and friendship. As joyful as that picnic was, imagine how much more joyful it could've been if we had thought to invite the folks from the neighboring low-income apartment complex, the folks from the area group homes, and maybe even the recently arrived immigrant families. Imagine how much more it would have reflected Jesus' vision of an open and welcoming faith community. Maybe the next time we have a parish gathering, we should let Jesus help us make out the guest list.

Jesus challenges us to invite the uninvited to our homes and our churches because He wants us to know them, not just know *about* them. He wants us to see them as persons, not just as statistics or projects. And by inviting them into our presence, and laughing, talking, and eating with them, we, who might see ourselves as more comfortable and self-sufficient, can learn from them. We will discover that they have a greater dependence on God, a greater openness to God's presence and power in their lives, than many of us do. And this may help us see that we are not as self-sufficient as we thought. We are all lowly beggars, sustained only by the mercy and grace of a sovereign God. Father Dan reminded us in his homily two weeks ago, that every single thing we have is a gift from God — pure grace — not something we earned or deserve. And most of us know how quickly it can all be taken from us. As Christians we are commanded to share these gifts us with those who are less fortunate. The words of Jesus in today's Gospel passage and throughout all of the Gospels make it crystal clear. IT IS NOT AN OPTION!

We often hear the question, "Where is God when it hurts?" The answer to that question is another question: "Where is the Church when it hurts?" We are the Church, the followers of Jesus Christ; we are God's primary response to the suffering and needs of the world. It is in recognition of this responsibility that our parish has instituted the new Sharing Program as a way we can give back to God in thanksgiving for what God has given us. In this Sharing Program, a fixed percentage of our weekly collections — taken right off the top — will be given to organizations and projects that help people in need. This year it will be a modest 2.5%. Eventually we hope to raise this to ten percent — the Biblical standard of tithing. The details of how the Sharing Program will work have been covered in the last several issues of the bulletin, and Father Ed will talk about all this next week. What I've been asked to do is to give a few examples — from my own experience — of the kinds of organizations and projects whose work with the poor and marginalized can benefit from the blessings we will share with them.

One that I have been associated with for quite some time is the House of Mercy. It is a community center on Hudson Avenue that provides a wide range of services to the inner city's poor. It is run by three Sisters of Mercy and one paid staff person assisted by volunteers from within the community it serves. On any day if you happen to walk in you might see folks gathered in the main room socializing over coffee and donuts or rummaging through piles of donated clothing, or they might be celebrating a Eucharistic liturgy, or waiting in line for the weekly food distribution. At the same time, the Sisters are in their offices helping individuals with their housing, employment, and health care problems, or guiding them through the maze of Social Service regulations or arranging to get them into drug or alcohol rehabilitation programs, or signing them up for special tutoring classes. To say that it's a busy place would be a gross understatement. In order to provide all these services to close to four thousand people a year, the House of Mercy depends mainly on the generous contributions of its supporters.

St. Bridget's Church is a very small, very poor, yet very spirit-filled parish in downtown Rochester. The pastor, Father Tony Mugavero, and a core group of about one hundred families have been laboring for several years to keep the parish alive and keep its spiritual and educational programs going while contending with a Church building that's in a drastic state of structural decay. I remember when we took our youth group down there to help clean and paint some of the parish buildings, and as we walked through the church building and saw how badly the walls and ceiling were crumbling, I wondered if the ushers had to hand out hard hats along with hymnals as people came to Mass. Father Tony and the St. Bridget's faith community sorely need the financial help of outside benefactors if they are going to have a safe and sound place to come together to worship God.

The word 'cephas' is the Hebrew word for rock or foundation (St. Paul in his letters sometimes used Cephas when referring to Peter). Cephas is also the name of a non-profit organization based in Rochester dedicated to helping men and women in prison and on parole. Cephas leaders and volunteers conduct weekly group counseling sessions for hundreds of inmates in prisons in western New York. I've sat in on a couple of these sessions at Attica Correctional Facility with a group of "lifers." Believe me these group sessions are heavy-duty straight talk — no coddling — no BS. During these sessions, inmates learn to confront the attitudes and behaviors that are responsible for their being where they are, and they work hard to restructure their thinking and attitudes so that they can manage their lives more effectively when they get out. Cephas continues to help inmates after their release from prison with room and board, and job-training at one of the Cephas residences. The success of this prison ministry is reflected in the fact that 70% of those who complete the rigorous Cephas program go on to live as productive, tax-paying citizens. To sustain this ministry, Cephas depends on profits from its construction business and on the generosity of individuals and organizations who want to see this vital ministry continued.

These are just a few examples of the many, many groups and organizations who work among and for the needy, making a difference in their lives, letting them know that God loves and cares for them. We can make a difference too, both as a parish — through our Sharing Program — and as individuals as we reflect on God's goodness in our lives and consider our personal responsibility to those less fortunate than ourselves.

Many of you, I am sure are like me. You look around and see all of the suffering and poverty and misery in our world — even right here in our community — and you turn to God in exasperation and ask, "If you're such a loving, merciful God, how can you see all of this suffering and not do anything about it?" But if we listen deep in our hearts, I think we can hear God's answer: "I have done something about it; I made you." AMEN.

CONNECTING TO THE WORD

1. List some Christ-like qualities. Do you see these
    qualities in anyone you know ? Do you see these
    qualities in someone you know as an acquaintance
    and would like to know better? Imagine that you
    are having a dinner party. Make a list of guests.
    Each guest should be put on the list because he
    or she has one or more of the Christ-like qualities
    that you listed. Don't forget to include yourself.

2. Do you consider yourself as a person on the A-
    list in life ? If so, do you offer your hospitality
    only to other people on the A-list or do you also
    offer it to those who have not been invited into
    society? Do you offer welcome to people from
    all walks of life? If so, have you ever been ostra-
    cized for doing so?

3. Do you consider yourself on the B- list — an
    outsider who is being passed by? If you feel on
    the outskirts of society, what factors in your life or
    community created this place for you? Have you
    ever thought of reaching out to others who also
    feel left out? How can those who feel forgotten
    get together to make an B-list of their own?

4. Where is God when life hurts? He dwells in the
    gifts he has given to each of us. In your mind
    unwrap the gift of life that God has granted you
    and look at what is inside. What has God given to

you? Have you used any of these gifts when life has been difficult — when you have felt pain and hurt within?

5. Where is the Church when it hurts? Does your church population reflect only the strong? Is there a place for economically, spiritually, and physically challenged persons? Are there opportunities in your parish for the economically, spiritually, and physically healthy to share their resources with those who are struggling?

6. What gifts do you bring to your Church? Have your gifts been offered but ignored? If so, are you willing to offer them again? Have you ever encouraged others to share their gifts? If so, was the reaction positive, negative, or mixed? If they did open up and share their gifts, was it an immediate or a gradual offering?

7. Make a list of short-term and long-term projects that will diversify your church's membership. Make a list of immediate and long-term projects that you, as an individual, are willing to join in order to reach out to others who are feeling forgotten or left out.

TWENTY-SEVENTH SUNDAY OF ORDINARY TIME - YEAR C

Habakuk 1:2-3, 2:2-4; 2Timothy 1:6-8, 13-14;
Luke 17:5-10

Lord, Increase My Faith

I've always liked those movies and television shows where the characters can travel backward or forward in time. I'm always intrigued by what it would have been like to have lived long ago, or what it's going to be like living well into the future. Let's suppose you could climb into a time machine and get transported back into the year 1776. And suppose you brought with you a copy of today's newspaper and showed it to some people there in 1776. Do you think they'd have a hard time making any sense of it? They would probably ask you to explain certain words like: automobile, airplane, cell phones, TV, spaceship, computers, world-wide web, and many more. After hearing your explanations, what do you think they'd say? They'd probably say something like, "You're out of your mind. Anybody with any sense knows that things like that are impossible" It would be no big surprise if a lot of what the people of one century consider normal and commonplace, was never even dreamed of by people of an earlier century.

Now let's go in the other direction and set our time machine to exactly one hundred years from today. Suppose once we get there we log on to the Internet to read our favorite newspaper. As we scan the news, we are astonished by the absence of any stories about violence, or crime; nothing about wars or conflicts between nations; no mention of poverty or racism or injustice; no pictures of anti-abortion protesters; no editorials on euthanasia; and not a single word about October 4th being Respect Life Sunday because it is no longer needed. The paper contains only stories of peace, prosperity, friendship, and love. What would we say? Probably something like: "There's something wrong with this machine — it must've gotten messed up and taken us into some fantasy world that can't ever happen. Anybody with any sense knows wherever there are people there will be violence and hostility and injustice. We will never have a world where there is total respect for human life."

There's an important lesson here. If we approach life with the belief that peace on earth is impossible, that at heart people are selfish and uncaring, that violence and aggression will always be used to deal with conflicts , then we will never have a world that is any different than what we have now. It may even get worse. But we don't have to think this way. Peace on earth IS possible. Love among all people IS possible. Respect for all life IS possible. And the reason these are possible is that Jesus came among us and taught us how to live. He showed us they were possible. We just haven't caught on yet. He said these things were possible when he taught us to pray to the Father, "Thy kingdom come, Thy will be done, on earth as it is in Heaven."

We pray this over and over, yet most of us would need a huge boost of faith to believe that God's kingdom could actually be realized on earth. We've forgotten what faith is all about — forgotten what God can accomplish. Like the Apostles in today's Gospel, we cry out, "Lord, increase our faith! If You want us to do what You've commanded; if You want us to share Your vision of what is possible, You'll have to strengthen our faith."

That's what we need. Lord, just increase our faith, then we'll be able to do what You ask. We'll be able to fully embrace the Church's teaching on the dignity and value of all life — especially the lives of those most vulnerable, those unable to speak for themselves... Increase our faith, Lord, and we will speak out against what Pope John Paul called the "culture of death" and say *no* to what many in our society condone: *no* to snuffing out the lives of the unborn, and *yes* to adoption and programs to support pregnant women; *no* to euthanasia and assisted suicide and *yes* to loving care for the sick until they die naturally... Increase our faith, Lord, and we will say *no* to the death penalty and *yes* to life sentences without parole. We will say *no* to unjust economic structures and policies that keep millions of lives forever mired in poverty, and *yes* to reforming our economic systems... Increase our faith and we will say *no* to military actions and wars that destroy innocent lives, *no* to weapons of destruction and *yes* to destruction of weapons... Increase our faith and we will say *no* to hatred and hostility toward people of different races, religions and ethnic backgrounds and *yes* to respecting and appreciating the goodness, the gifts and the lives of all your people.

Increase our faith, Lord, and not only will we speak out, but we will take action to protect and defend all life. We won't stand on the sidelines and let others fight the battles. We will work to influence public debate and policies on these life issues. We will write letters to the Governor and the President and our lawmakers. We'll sign petitions and join in peaceful protest marches. We'll find out which candidates consistently support life and vote for them, maybe even work for them... Increase our faith, Lord, and we'll volunteer wherever we can to support life: soup kitchens, AIDS clinics, hospices, problem pregnancy centers... Increase our faith, Lord, and we'll exercise leadership in business to change policies and practices that burden the lives of low-income workers and their families... Increase our faith and we'll dig deeper to give more of the gifts you have given us to help lift up our brothers and sisters in need.

We could do all these things, Lord, if you would just give us more faith. And how does Jesus answer us? The same way he answered the Apostles: "If you have faith the size of a mustard seed, you would say to this mulberry tree, 'Be uprooted and planted in the sea,' and it would obey you." In other words, if we had even the tiniest bit of faith, we could do all these things, we could accomplish what now seems impossible." What Jesus is telling us is that we don't need *more* faith than we already have. It's just that our faith is misdirected. Too many of us look at ourselves instead of God. We look at ourselves and say, "I can't do it. I'm not strong enough, loving enough, giving enough, faithful enough to do it." We're right. We don't have what it takes. But, my friends, God does. God has the power. And our faith — our puny little faith — links us to that power, the same power which Jesus, in his life and death, clearly and powerfully demonstrated over and over again. God's power working through our faith — individually and as a community — can accomplish even the seemingly impossible goal of making all human life respected, valued and safe.

We have to stop making excuses for doing too little, stop blaming our lack of faith. Jesus assures us the faith we have is more than enough. We have to stop making the excuse that the task is too overwhelming, that we can't see how our meager efforts can make any difference. When we start thinking that way, let's remember this: *the woods and the trees would be very silent if the only birds singing were the ones that sing the best* …So go and work with the faith you have. Use that mustard seed faith to do just one or two of the things I suggested and trust God's power to do the rest. Who knows? If enough of us do it, the day may come when we will be able to pray to the Father: Thy kingdom *has* come, Thy will *has* been done on earth as it is in heaven. AMEN.

CONNECTING TO THE WORD

1. How have you said "Yes" to life? List specific examples. How have you said "No" to life? List specific examples. Is it easier to say "Yes" or to say "No"? Has anyone or any event in your life moved you towards a "No" or a "Yes" stance in the fight for life?

2. Do your representatives in office say "Yes" or "No" to life? Who are your local, state, and federal representatives? Have you written to any of them to share your views for life to them? If not why haven't you? If you have, what was their response?

3. Do you exercise your right to vote? Do you cast your ballot for those who support life? Are there some life issues you regard as more important than others when you select a candidate?

4. Do you feel powerless on earth? Have you acknowledged that your faith can be a source of power? Would you prefer to remain powerless? If so, why? Do you use your faith as a source of power? If so, how? Have you encouraged those around you to do this as well?

5. Do you stay quiet in the forest of believers or are you vocal? Do you associate with vocal believers without speaking yourself? As you see it, what are specific battles for life that the human race

faces? Have any of them been championed? Has the fight begun for any of these issues? Are some of these issues left untouched by us?

6. Say the *Our Father* slowly. As you do so, reflect on what its words truly mean. What can you and I do to help begin to bring God's will — God's vision — to fruition here on earth? Make a resolution to take at least two or three of the life-respecting actions called for in the homily. Set a timetable, and hold yourself accountable. Try to enlist others to go along with you.

TWENTY-NINTH OF ORDINARY TIME - YEAR C

*Exekiel 17:8-13; 2 Timothy 3:14-4:2; **Luke 18:1-8***

You Can Make A Difference

In the ten years I've been preaching, I've learned that no matter how clear and understandable I try to be, there's always someone who hears something different than what I said. This happens a lot in our everyday communication. I saw a comic strip recently that showed some examples of this. A mother has just met her daughter's new fiancé. What she actually says to her daughter is: "If you're happy, dear, I'm happy." But what the daughter hears is: "I can't believe you want to marry this loser." Then there is the picture of a husband and wife all dressed up to go out. He says to her: "Honey, you look pretty tonight." But what the wife hears is: "Most of the time you look old and fat." What a listener hears isn't always what the speaker said. That's often the case with the parable Jesus used in today's passage from Luke's Gospel.

It's about a widow who had been wronged and she goes to court to get justice but the judge ignores her. Apparently the judge was the kind who only responded to bribes or other favors which the poor widow couldn't offer. He keeps ignoring the woman, but there she is every day, pestering him, pleading her case. Eventually she wears him down, and the dishonest judge grants her the justice she deserves. The message people tend to hear in this parable is that if you pray hard enough and long enough, you'll eventually wear God down and He'll give you what you ask for. But is that really what Jesus was saying? I don't think so. Praying hard and long is good for us to do — for reasons I'll go into another time — but we all know from experience that it won't always get us what we ask for. Oh sure, God will answer our prayers, but the answer won't always be the one we want, because God knows that sometimes what we're asking for isn't the right thing for us. If God had answered my persistent, pleading prayers when I was a young man, I would've ended up married to the wrong woman. Thank you, God for knowing better!

To understand what this parable is saying, we can't look at it as an isolated story. You see, Luke put this parable where it is for a reason. He put it right after a section where Jesus talks to His disciples about His Second Coming and how they would long for the day when He would return, because they knew that on that day the Son of God would vanquish the forces of evil and bring justice to the earth. Now Luke knew that the early Christians He was writing for were suffering persecution and injustices. They were getting more and more discouraged as each day went by without Jesus returning. So Luke inserts this parable which Jesus uses to "show them that they should pray always and not lose heart."

It's clear from the context that Jesus is talking about a specific prayer request. The widow in the parable comes asking for justice — not anything else. Not a new husband, not a healing for herself or a loved one. She comes seeking justice. Now widows in that society were as helpless as helpless can be. They had no power, no resources. Yet, Jesus has her pitted against this unsympathetic judge who represents the unbending power structures of society. Jesus holds her up as a model of persistence for His followers. He wants them to pray to God to bring justice to His people, pray to God to help them persevere, hang in there and continually work for justice in an unjust world, with confidence that God is working with them until the day Jesus comes back to make all things right.

It's important here to define what the term "justice" means when it is used in the Bible. Biblical justice refers to putting things right, putting things back to how God intended them to be at the Creation. God intended for every human being to share in the *gifts* of creation, to have everything they needed to live and to love and to build and to grow to their full potential — and then we went and messed it all up. From the beginning, human actions have transformed the perfect world God created into a broken world in which there are many people who are left out, who do not share in these gifts, who may not even have their basic needs being met. Biblical justice means to take action to fix this brokenness, to work to change the conditions in society that produce it. Get things back to the way God meant them to be.

Biblical justice is built on the essential worth and dignity of every single person from the moment they were conceived in the womb. One of the major Catholic social documents reminds us that human dignity is not something one earns by their achievements. The single mother who slings burgers at McDonald's so her children can eat, the migrant farm-worker toiling in the fields, the child with a swollen belly scavenging through a garbage dump in a third-world country, share the same human dignity as the Nobel prize winner, the television celebrity, the people teaching our children. There is a unique and sacred worth that is present in *every* person simply because she or he has been created by God, has been made in the image and likeness of God. Because of this shared human dignity, we who call ourselves Christians have a responsibility to the poor, the oppressed, the exploited, the powerless — those who are so often treated as less valued, less worthy. It is our responsibility to help change the unjust structures and institutions and practices that create or contribute to their suffering.

When Jesus calls His followers to a prayerful, active, justice-seeking faith, it is nothing new. If you were to take the time to read through the entire Bible, you would find the term "justice" occurs over 130 times. If you were to move through the Bible, you would be struck by how often God sticks up for the little guy, the disadvantaged person, the one holding the short end of the stick. Again and again, God calls

His people to watch out for, to care for, the poor, the widow, the orphan, the alien (see Deuteronomy 24:17-22). Again and again, through the words of prophets like Isaiah and Micah, Amos and Jeremiah, God makes clear our responsibility not only to act justly ourselves, but to work to eliminate injustices against those powerless to do it for themselves. And of course, we have Jesus Himself warning us that we will be judged on how we treat the least among us.

My friends, when it comes to economics, resources, opportunities, medical care, most of us sit comfortably near the top of the mountain, while millions of our brothers and sisters live way beneath us on a few dollars a day. It's hard for us — unless we've been there — to know what life looks like from the bottom. So, we have to continually educate ourselves about the works of justice. The mainstream media certainly isn't going to do it. Their job is to push us into buying a new car, drinking more beer, or going on the latest, greatest diet. It is up to us to seek out the voices of those at the bottom, and listen to them, find out how we can help them. I'm not talking about throwing a few extra cans into our food collection basket, or writing a check for our Mercy Fund, or cooking a meal for our homeless guests. These are all good things. Please keep doing them. Right now, they are needed. I'm talking about helping to bring about changes so that someday those kinds of things won't be needed.

How do we do this? First, by keeping informed. Read about Social Justice issues in our bulletin articles and inserts, and in the handouts we put out in the foyer. Come and listen when we have speakers here or at area churches or at St. Bernard's. Get on the Internet and search under *Catholic Social Justice* for scads of information. Go on the Project URGE Bus Tour to see firsthand the works of Social Justice being done in Rochester. Then, take action. Study and sign petitions that will go to government officials and lawmakers. Write letters and send e-mails to the President and Congress, the Governor, state legislators. Maybe get on the bus to Albany to lobby for justice. Be like that persistent widow; hammer away until they listen. Find out which candidates will work to correct injustices, and vote for them — maybe even work for them. If you run a business, lead by example with policies and practices that improve the lives of low-income workers and their families. You can do any of these on your own, or better still as a project for your RENEW group.

At the end of today's Gospel, Jesus asks: "...when the Son of Man comes, will He find faith on earth?" That's a question each of us should take personally. I know I do. When Jesus comes for me — at the end of my life or on the last day — do I want Him to find a man whose faith was a "that's just the way things are" kind of faith? Do I just throw up my hands and tell Him, "Lord, there was just too much wrong in the world, it was too overwhelming. I can't see how anything I could've done would've made a difference."? Or do I want Him to find a man who lived as if the word "faith" was a verb, not a noun. A man who believed that even his meager efforts were part of God's ultimate plan to bring divine justice to the earth, to make all things right? I know which one I want. Now — with the Lord's help — I have to go and live it. I pray that each of you do the same. AMEN.

CONNECTING TO THE WORD

1. Sometimes our prayers are answered in ways we don't realize. Do you have any unanswered prayers nested in your heart? Make of list of things you have prayed for or for which you are currently praying. Take a look at your list. With the passing of time, have some of your prayers become less relevant? Have some of your prayers been answered? If some of the prayers on your list remain relevant and unanswered, is there someone to whom you can reach out for spiritual guidance as you search for answers to your prayers?

2. If you are seeking something specific like the woman in the gospel, reflect on what you need (e.g., strength, courage, wisdom) to patiently work towards the attainment of your heart's longing.

3. Do you know of a family, parish, school, or individual currently in need of help but you do not know what you personally can contribute to the situation? If so, speak to a social ministry person at your parish or in your community. Ask them their advice regarding how you may be of service in this situation. If it is not appropriate for you to become personally involved, add the situation to your prayer list.

SPECIAL LITURGIES

TRINITY SUNDAY – YEAR C

Proverbs 8:22-31; Romans 5:1-5; John 16:12-15

Who's On First?[1]

Whenever Holy Trinity Sunday comes around, I find myself thinking: "Boy, God sure has a sense of humor." I'm convinced that on Trinity Sunday God is getting a big kick out of watching preachers all over the world struggle to explain the unexplainable: the great mystery of God, the Father, the Son and the Holy Spirit – three persons, yet one God – with each person fully and totally God. Well, I decided that God isn't going to get a laugh at my expense, so I won't be trying to explain the Trinity. But, I thought since God has such a great sense of humor, He wouldn't mind if I had a little fun imagining one of the great comedy teams of all time — Bud Abbot and Lou Costello — and how they would have handled explaining the Trinity. I think Bud and Lou might've done it something like this:

Lou (he's the short chubby one): Hey, Bud, you're pretty smart. I bet you know a lot about religion.
Bud: Well, yes Lou, I do. What would you like to know?

Lou: I drove past a church today. It had a big sign that said "Holy Trinity Church". You know, Bud, I've seen churches named St. Peter, St. Paul, and St. Joseph, but I never heard of St. Trinity. Who is this St. Trinity?

Bud: Lou, Trinity is not a saint. Trinity is the way that Christians have come to understand God as revealed to us in the Bible. The Trinity is God. One God in Three Persons: God the Father, God the Son and God the Holy Spirit.

Lou: That sure sounds like three gods to me.

Bud: No, Lou, one God, three persons. It's a mystery Lou.

Lou: Hmm. One God, three persons… Come to think of it, this is a very big world and there are lots of people for God to watch. So probably the Father works the day shift, the Son the night shift and the Holy Spirit the graveyard shift.

Bud: Uh, no, Lou. There are no shifts. God's working all of the time.

Lou: OK. So if God's working all the time, it's still a very big world, so maybe God divides the world into thirds. You know, a third for the Father, a third for the Son and a third for the Holy Spirit.

Bud: No, Lou, no thirds, no divisions. God is undivided.

Lou: I still don't get it… Let me ask it to you this way, Bud. I think God must be a big baseball fan. After all, the first words of the Bible say "In the big inning."

Bud: No, no, Lou, it's "In the beginning" not "In the big inning."

Lou:. Oh. Anyway, God must be a big baseball fan; He invented it. So let's say that God's team is playing a baseball game and God's team is up to bat. The Father is up first, and He hits a single. Tell me, Bud, who's on first?

Bud: God.

Lou: The Father.

Bud: That's right, Lou.

Lou: OK. Now the Son comes up and He hits a single and God goes to second base. Now, who's on first?

Bud: .God.

Lou: Wait a minute...I thought God was on second base.

Bud: That's right. God is on second.

Lou: Ooh, I'm getting so confused... Now let's say the Holy Spirit comes up to bat and lays down a perfect bunt. The Father goes to third base, the Son goes to second base and the Holy Spirit beats out the throw — safe at first! Now, who's on first?

Bud: God.

Lou: But you just told me God was on second and third.

Bud: That's right Lou. God is on second and third. God is on first too. God is on all the bases. The bases are loaded with God.

Lou: This is getting more confusing by the minute. If there's only one God, how can God be on all three bases?

Bud: God can do anything.

Lou: Well, if God can do anything, why doesn't He make Himself easier for us to understand?

Bud: I don't know, Lou. I'm sure He has good reasons. But, don't worry about trying to understand the Trinity. Just be thankful that God has made Himself known to us and is here with us, even if we can't quite figure Him out.

Many of us are like Lou. We want an explanation that makes sense, but believe me there isn't any. The Trinity isn't a mystery we need to solve; the Trinity is a gift we should celebrate. So, I'm with Bud. I think we should get on our knees every day in thanks and gratitude that our God isn't a remote, hands-off kind of God, floating around in outer space, letting us stumble along on our own. No, our God — the God of the Holy Trinity — can't stay away from us. Why? Because our lives matter to God. What happens to us matters to God. We see that throughout Scripture, from the Father's work of creation to the Son's living and dying as one of us, to the Holy Spirit's coming at Pentecost. And, our God is no solitary God. Our God — though One — is a family, a community of three persons bound together by their love for one another. A love so great, so perfect, so powerful, that God wants to share it with His creation. This mutual love of Father, Son and Holy Spirit for one another overflows to each of us, is poured out into our hearts as Paul tells us in our second reading, draws us into the inner circle of God's family, and calls us to share in the life of the Holy Trinity. That's what God wants — to share His life with us. God wants a relationship with us. Moses told the people that way back in the beginning. Jesus preached it over and over. God wants to be in our life, right here in the nitty-gritty, down here in the trenches with us, in the suffering, in the fears, in every crisis and cross, and in every joy and triumph and victory.

And so, my friends, as we celebrate the Holy Trinity, each of us needs to ask, "How am I doing? How am I doing in my relationship with God? Have I really let God into my life in all the ways God has made Himself available to me — as Father, as Son, and as Holy Spirit? Now, I suspect — if we're honest — many of us know we can do a lot better. Our lives may be so busy, rushing from one activity to the next, or we're so loaded down with obligations and responsibilities – work, family, school, sports – or we just don't give God a high priority until we get socked with some unexpected crisis. Whatever it is, we haven't let God be at the center of our life; instead we've kept Him out there flapping around on the edges.

If this sounds like where you're at right now, I have a practical suggestion to help make the Trinity a bigger part of your life. And it takes only about three minutes just before you fall asleep at night. Here's what you do:

During the first minute, think about the good things that happened to you that day. Maybe you handled a tough situation well. Maybe you enjoyed a pleasant walk along the canal. Then **talk to the**

Father about all these good things, and thank Him for them.

During the second minute, pick out the low point of your day, something you wish hadn't happened — like a shouting match you had with your child, or your parent , or a temptation you gave in to. Then **talk to Jesus** about it. Ask Him to forgive you, and promise Him you'll try to handle it His way next time.

During the third minute, look ahead to the next day. Is there some critical situation or task you need to face and you're not sure how to handle it? **Talk to the Holy Spirit** about it. Ask the Spirit to be there with you, to lead you and guide you to do what you need to do. Then, go to sleep. That's it. Pretty simple, huh? But by making this time with the Trinity part of your daily routine, you'll be bringing God smack into the middle of your day to day life, right where God wants to be.

Getting back to the baseball scenario, we can think of it like this: If God is on first, second and third base, it's up to us to pick up the bat, step into the batter's box and bring God home, bring God into our life. God gives us the free will to say yes or no, and gives us the grace and the faith to decide to pick up that bat, step up to the plate and start swinging. The beauty of it is that God loves us so much that as long as we are willing to stay up there and keep swinging, God will let us stay there as long as it takes. There's no "three strikes and you're out!" Sure, there are times when we will swing and miss the ball, and times when we'll hit a foul ball, but with God's help if we keep swinging, eventually we'll connect. We'll get hold of the right pitch and clear the bases and bring God fully home into our lives. Then, if we're ever asked, "Who's on first in your life," we will be able to answer without any hesitation, "God...God's on first." AMEN.

CONNECTING TO THE WORD

1. Has a small child ever asked you to explain the unexplainable? If a child's pet has just died, how would you try to get him/her to understand? What images and/or concepts would you use?

2. St. Patrick used the three-leaf clover, and this homily used the Abbot and Costello routine to describe the Holy Trinity. Do you have a favorite way to understand the Trinity or explain it to others?

3. Who or what is on first base in your life? If it isn't God, why do you think that is so? How would your life be different if you put God on first? What do you need to do to have that happen?

4. Take a few minutes right now to pray to the Trinity using the method described in the homily:

    (a) Recall all the good things that happened to you in the last 24 hours. Say a prayer of thanksgiving to God the Father.

    (b) Recall the low point of the last 24 hours. Talk to Jesus about it.

    (c) Think ahead to what you need to do in the next 24 hours. Pray to the Holy Spirit for guidance.

NOTES

1. A great deal of credit for adapting the classic Abbot and Costello routine ,"Who's On First?", goes to Al Schifano's sermon of May 2002 on *www.sermoncentral.com* .

BODY AND BLOOD OF CHRIST (CORPUS CHRISTI) - YEAR C

Genesis 14:18-20; 1Corinthians 11:23-26;
Luke 9:11-17

What Shall I Do Lord? What... Shall... I ... Do?

There was once an old man who had lived a good and holy life, but in his declining years he felt that he had nothing to show for it. So he decided to ask God for a miracle. He fell to his knees and prayed: "Lord, I've been a good man all my life. I've never asked You for anything before, and I'm grateful for all you've given me. So please, Lord, grant me one request. Let me win the lottery." Days passed and nothing happened, so again he prayed to win the lottery. Still nothing. After months of praying and praying with no success, the old man cried out to heaven, "God, will you give me a break? All I'm asking is, let me win the lottery!"... Suddenly a voice thundered from the sky, "Old man, will you give Me a break? At least buy a ticket!"

God can work miracles without any help from us, but He likes it better when we do at least a little something on our end — when we at least buy a ticket.

Like in today's Gospel story. Jesus could've fed those thousands of hungry people on the hillside without the five loaves and the two fish, and without the assistance of his disciples, but He chose to use all of them as part of the miracle. And it's the same with the miracle we are celebrating and experiencing today on this Feast of the Body and Blood of Christ — the miracle we celebrate and experience at every Mass.

When Christ feeds us with the food that gives new and everlasting life, the food that is His Body and Blood, He gives us this incredible, mysterious, life-giving gift with an important string attached. It must be shared. If we partake of the Eucharist, then we must become Eucharist for others; we must be part of bringing the miracle of the Eucharist — the unlimited, compassionate love of Christ — to people and places that hunger for it. Like the disciples who helped Jesus with the multiplication of the loaves and fish, we must help Christ with the multiplication of the Eucharist.

Put another way, the Real Presence of Christ in the Eucharist is not just for our own personal benefit, to heal our brokenness, to strengthen us for our day to day struggles and challenges. Sure, that's part of it, but there's a lot more. In the words of Pope Pius XII, "If you have received worthily, you are what you have received." The Real Presence of Christ in the consecrated bread and cup becomes Christ present in us as we eat and drink and then move from the Eucharistic table to go back out into the world. As St. Paul exclaimed in his letter to the Galatians, "It is no longer I who live; Christ lives in me!"

This feast of the Body and Blood of Christ challenges us to not keep the Christ who lives in us all to ourselves. We must carry the Christ who lives in us to our little acre of God's world. We are the ones who must bring the Eucharist — the Real Presence of Christ — to every dark corner of that acre...We are the ones who bring the Real Presence of Christ to those who are in pain: the neighbor whose spouse died so suddenly; the couple whose marriage has just fallen apart; the old man forced to leave his home and fifty years of memories behind. It is our concern and compassion that lets them know the love of Christ in their pain.

We are the ones who bring the Real Presence of Christ to those who are sad and lonely: in a nursing home, in the hospital, in their home, in prison. Our visits and our kindness show them that Christ has not forgotten them.

We are the ones who bring Christ to those who are overwhelmed by what life has thrown at them and who feel like they can't make it through another day. Not too long ago, I visited a man who feels just this way. He told me, "You know, it's the worst when I wake up in the morning and I have to face everything again. I almost wish I didn't wake up." When we give our help or even just a listening heart to people struggling under their burdens, we're making Christ's invitation real to them: "Come to me all who are weary and heavy burdened, and I will give you rest."

We are the ones who bring Christ to those who are afraid: the patient who's just been told, "There's nothing more we can do for you"; the parents whose son or daughter is heavily into drugs; the widow who is on her own for the first time in her life. When we comfort and encourage those who are anxious or fearful, we help them feel the closeness of Christ holding them and reassuring them: "Take heart, it is I. Do not be afraid."

We become the Real Presence of Christ when we share our blessings and resources with those who have less than we do. When we give of our time and energy in outreach projects like the Soup Kitchen and Habitat for Humanity, we are making present and real Christ's special love and concern for the poor.

When we take a firm stand against prejudice and discrimination, when we speak out in opposition to violence in all its forms, when we advocate for peace and justice in all areas of life, we are letting the Real Presence of Christ - his peace and his passion for justice - shape the society in which we live.

And all of you young people, especially our new graduates, who we will honor with a special blessing a little later, how about you? Empowered by the Eucharist, the Christ who lives in you, you too can do all these things to bring the Real Presence of Christ where it is needed. But on top of that, you have a special mission that the rest of us don't have, because your world is a little different than ours. And it's not an easy mission; it could bring you ridicule or rejection or both. Your mission is to say, "No" to drugs, "No" to alcohol, "No, not now" to sexual activity, and "Yes" to God, "Yes" to your faith. In doing this you will be a strong witness to Christ's love and concern for the well-being of young people in a way that can have a tremendous influence on your peers.

What I have been trying to say to old and young alike — what today's feast of the Body and Blood of Christ should remind us — is that our Eucharistic celebration is not only about our eating and drinking of the precious Body and Blood; it is also about what we do after we leave here, having partaken of the Sacred Meal. As people of faith, if we truly believe that Christ comes to us in the Eucharist, that Christ lives in us, then we should ask ourselves, "Where I work, where I spend my day, with my family... are these places different, better, more filled with Christ because I am there?"

If my words have failed to help you see the ways you are called to be the Real Presence of Christ when you go out the church door today, then I suggest that as you come forward to receive Christ in a few minutes, simply repeat the words of Paul as he was knocked to the ground on the road to Damascus. Simply ask the Christ within you, "What shall I do Lord? ... What ... shall ... I ... do?" AMEN!

CONNECTING TO THE WORD

1. In your deepest moments of weariness have you had your burden lightened, or have you ever lightened another's burden during a difficult time?

2. Consider Christ as the one who gives shape to our lives. Do you use His example to frame your actions or do you live outside of it, resisting His embrace, wondering where He is in your life?

3. List several qualities of Christ. Has He blessed you with any of these traits? Have you recognized any of these traits in a friend, neighbor or loved one?

4. Have you ever asked Christ for guidance? After making this brave inquiry what was His reply? Did He send His message through an event or person? Has Christ ever sent a message through you? If so, what allowed you to hear Him? Was His message warmly passed on and receptively received?

ALL SOUL'S DAY

*Isaiah 25:6-9; **John 14:1-6***

Good Luck In Your New Location

Today we celebrate All Souls Day as we remember and pray for those who have gone before us. I'd like to start with this little story. The vice president of a bank was opening a new branch office, and a friend of his had sent a lovely wreath of flowers for the grand opening. But when the friend arrived at the grand opening, she was appalled to find that the wreath she had sent bore the inscription, *Rest in Peace*. When she called the florist to complain, the florist said he was very sorry; he had mixed up the flowers sent to the bank with flowers sent to a funeral. Then, trying to calm the angry customer, he said, "You think you feel bad. Somewhere today there's a guy lying in a casket under a wreath of flowers that says, *Good Luck In Your New Location.*"

Good luck in your new location. This kind of ties in with what happened the other day when I stopped to look at some old family photographs hanging on our living room wall. I pass by these pictures probably twenty times a day, but every now and then I find myself studying those faces from the past. There's Grampa Tocci — the stern family patriarch. I never knew him. There's Uncle Lee, who barely spoke more than ten words a day, but he could get any motor or engine to purr like a kitten. Look, there's cousin Rose — the family blabbermouth. And that delicate, little flower with the Mona Lisa smile, that's the other Rose, my mother. She died when I was only two. And there's my Dad and Uncle Sam and all those other dear people from my earlier life. As my eyes scanned all those faces, I remember feeling a little sad because most of them are gone now, and I wondered "Where are they now? Where's *their* new location?"

Today's memorial of All Souls might find us wondering the same things as we call to mind people who have left this life — some long ago, some not so long ago. People whom we loved and who loved us. People who — in large or small part — helped form us into the persons we have become. As we honor their memory, it's only natural to ponder the questions that have been pondered since the dawn of history: Is there something after death? Or is this life all there is?

The Bible provides us with many assurances that there indeed is life after death, that there is an eternity of existence to look forward to (or in some cases not to look forward to). I find the words of Jesus in today's gospel especially promising. The scene takes place the night before He was to be put to death. Jesus has just told his friends that He would be leaving them, and they could not follow – at least not yet. Then He tells them about His Father's house and that He was going there — going on ahead to prepare a place for them – and He would come back to get them, to bring them home with Him.

His words reveal how differently Jesus looked at death compared to how we do. You and I often look at death from the back side. We see it only as a sad departure. It's like our friend or family member is on board a great sailing ship heading out to sea. And we are the ones left standing on the dock as the ship moves slowly out of sight. We wave good-bye for a long time. After a while, we wipe away our tears and get on with the business of living. Jesus looked at death from the other side. He saw death not as a departure, but as a homecoming.

That's how Jesus wants us to think about death. He wants us to see the view from the opposite shore — the distant shore toward which that mighty ship carrying our loved one is sailing. As the ship comes in, Jesus is there guiding our loved one ashore to where God the Father stands waiting, like the father in the Parable of the Prodigal Son, waiting with arms wide open..."Welcome home!"

In this gospel, Jesus assures us that if we have faith in the Father and faith in Him — and that means not only believing, but living what we believe — then there is a place He will personally take us to, a place where He is now, a place where none of us deserve to be except that Jesus died for us and took the punishment for our sins, a place we call heaven. Because Jesus is there, we can be sure heaven is a place of perfect peace and joy, love and life. It is the place of eternal happiness that the prophet Isaiah described in our first reading as a sumptuous feast, a banquet of food and drink beyond our wildest dreams, where death has no home and where the Lord God will wipe away the tears from every face. I also like the way St. Paul said it: "What eye has not seen, and ear has not heard, and what has not entered the human heart, what God has prepared for those who love Him. (1 Cor. 2:9) "

We have these promising words from Jesus, Isaiah, and Paul, and so many others throughout the Bible. If we believe these words, why then do we feel the need to pray for those who have died? If Christ's death has won for them life everlasting; if they believed in Christ as their savior and redeemer and tried to live according to His way, however imperfectly; if He has a place ready for them, then what can our prayers do? Why do we offer Mass for them over and over again? It's the same question a student asked in my High School religion class: "Why do we pray for the souls of the dead? If they're in heaven, they don't need our prayers; if they're in hell, all the prayers in the world aren't gonna help them. So, why pray for them?"

Because as Roman Catholics, yes, we believe that the souls of all who die in God's grace and friendship will go to heaven. But we also believe that — at death — no human soul is in the state of perfect holiness. In Matthew 5:48, Jesus says, "Be perfect as your heavenly Father is perfect." A soul must be perfect to live in the presence of an all holy, all perfect God. And so, any soul destined for heaven must first undergo a purification, a cleansing of all the residual effects of sin. To quote Pope John Paul II, "Before we enter into full communion with God, every trace of sin within us must be eliminated and every imperfection in our soul must be corrected."[1] We call this process of purification *purgatory*.

Purgatory is not a place, it's a process. How does this process take place and how long does it take? We don't know. Is it painful? Not in a physical sense because souls are not bodies; the pain is "spiritual". It is the pain of anguish and sorrow over the sin in our lives that delays our entrance into heaven... It is the deep, painful longing to see God, to be with God, of being so close, but not yet there. It is the pain of having to wait until we are made fit for heaven. The Church throughout history has prayed for and offered Mass for the souls of the dead to ease this spiritual suffering and move them more swiftly toward that state of perfect holiness when they will at long last gaze upon the Lord's beautiful and glorious face.

And so, on this memorial of All Souls, we pray for and offer the Holy Sacrifice of the Mass for all our beloved dead — those countless faces in the countless old photographs. We do this with faith and trust in the Lord's promise that one day He will bring each of us home to His Father's house, to that place He has prepared for us, to be reunited with all those who have gone before us, and to finally come face to face with the One who loves us most. May the souls of all the faithful departed, through the mercy of God, rest in peace... AMEN.

CONNECTING TO THE WORD

1. What are your images of heaven? What are your favorite Bible passages about heaven?

2. Can you still see your deceased loved ones vividly? Are the spiritual remnants of their love in your life?

3. What is your image of purgatory? In your heart, if you see your loved ones in purgatory, why are they there? Did they hurt you or those that you care about while they were on earth? Have you been able to forgive them and pray for them to expedite their entry into heaven?

4. How did your deceased loved ones show you their love while they were on earth? How did Jesus show His love to His friends and family while He was among us? How does He continue to show his love for us?

NOTES

1. From the pope's General Audience of Wednesday, 4 August 1999. Following his catecheses on heaven and hell, the Holy Father reflected on Purgatory.

LENTEN PENANCE SERVICE

Isaiah 1:16-18; Luke 15:1-3, 11-24

Thank You, Jesus, Thank You

True story. In 1979, 23 year-old Rusty Welborn of West Virginia was arrested following one of the most brutal killings in South Carolina history. Rusty was tried for murder and received the death penalty. Bob McAlister was a Christian who felt a strong call from God to minister to killers on death row. On Bob's first visit to Rusty's cell, he found Rusty lying on the floor, covered with dirt, not caring that roaches were crawling all over him. He was a pathetic picture of a man who believed he mattered to no one — that no one cared anything about him. As Bob talked to him, Rusty just stared blankly and didn't respond.

Visit after visit, Bob tried to reach Rusty, telling him how much Jesus loved him and that — even on death row — it wasn't too late for him to turn his life over to Christ. This went on for months. Bob would tell Rusty about Jesus, and Rusty would sit there, no reaction, until one day Bob read him today's Gospel about the Prodigal Son. Then Bob told him how Jesus had used the character of the father in the story to show us what God was really like. It was an image of

God totally foreign to Rusty. He had always thought of God as this vindictive judge, looking down from heaven, watching every move we make, ready to condemn us to eternal fire when we slip up. But in the parable, Jesus showed us God as the compassionate father who loves us even when we do terrible things — even when we run away from Him. A God who gives us the freedom to leave, but who watches and waits, hoping we will return. A God who waits for us to come to our senses and realize how miserable we are without Him, and when we come back humbly seeking forgiveness, promising to repent, He runs out to meet us, to welcome us back home.

This image of a loving, forgiving God began to gradually work on Rusty. He started to see himself differently. If God cared about him, he must be worth something. Little by little, he opened up, until one day he began to weep as Bob told him how Jesus had died on the cross for all sinners — even him — so that all sins — even murder — could be forgiven. On that day, Rusty Welborn, a vicious murderer, gave his heart to Jesus.

A few days later when Bob saw Rusty, he saw a new man. The cell was clean and so was Rusty. He had renewed energy and a positive outlook on life. A short time after that, Rusty begged for and received forgiveness for what he had done, not only from God, but from the family of the woman he had murdered. Bob continued to visit him, and during his last months, Rusty told Bob about his childhood in West Virginia. His family was dirt poor, and Rusty had been terribly abused and neglected. School had been an absolute nightmare both for him and for his teachers. Rusty quit school in ninth grade, and his teenage years were full of trouble as he was kicked out of his home many times and ran away countless others. He spent the better part of his youth living under bridges and in public rest rooms.

Rusty had never known real love in his life, and so he was absolutely amazed that other people — like Bob — could actually care about someone like him just because of their faith in Jesus Christ. Bob had taught Rusty a lot about God, and Rusty had taught Bob a lot about how to die. With only hours remaining before his execution, Rusty exhibited a calm and peaceful spirit like Bob had never seen before. He asked Bob to read to him from the Bible. After an hour or so of listening, Rusty sat up on the side of his cot and said, "You know, Bob, the only thing I ever wanted was a home. Now I'm going to get one."..Bob continued reading, and after a few minutes, Rusty grew very quiet. Thinking he had fallen asleep, Bob closed the Bible. As he turned to leave Rusty for the last time, he placed a blanket over him, tucked it in, and leaned over and kissed Rusty on the forehead...A short time later, Rusty Welborn was executed for murder.

A woman who had assisted Rusty in his final moments remembered the last words he spoke to her. As he was being prepared for his death, Rusty looked at her and said, "What a shame that a man's gotta wait 'til his last night alive to be kissed and tucked into bed for the very first time."

Rusty's story is a powerful reminder of why we are here, why we have come to this holy place. We are here because like Rusty we too are sinners — not murderers — but still sinners in need of God's mercy, God's forgiveness. I'll bet that — unlike Rusty — most of us have been kissed and tucked in many times. In a sense that's what will happen here in a few moments. God will kiss us, tuck us in, tell us that we are good, that we are loved, that we are forgiven, that nothing we have done or could ever do will make Him stop loving us.

It took Rusty a long time to finally believe this. Maybe some of us are having a hard time believing it too. We might be thinking, "What I've done is so bad, I just don't see how God can ever forgive me." Or maybe we just can't bring ourselves to promise that we'll make the changes God wants us to make to get our life on track because we're afraid we'll fall right back into the same sins. We need to realize that God doesn't expect us to be perfect. But He does expect us to keep trying. Falling down is not failing. Falling down and not getting back up — that's failing. And no matter how badly we fall, like Rusty and the Prodigal Son, we can come to God truly sorry, ready to admit our sins, ready to start over and try harder, and He'll be there waiting — arms open wide. All that bad stuff will be washed away as if it had never happened, just as the Lord promised in our first reading from Isaiah: "Cease doing evil; learn to do good... Though your sins be like scarlet, they will become white as snow." The slate will be wiped clean. We will start fresh — a new beginning.

Why does God give us chance after chance to start over? Why doesn't He just say, "Fine, if that's the way you want it, go ahead, live *your* way, but don't come running back to me later?" Why? Because — for reasons we may never know — God loves us too much to give us what we deserve. God loves us too much to let our sins separate us from Him forever. If you ever doubt this, you only need to look at the cross. Look at Jesus, our crucified Savior, look into those suffering eyes that cry out to us: "See how I love you. Do you understand *now* how much I love you? Can you ever, ever doubt my love for you?" Friends, being loved this much has to make a difference in our lives. It has to. It made a difference in Rusty's life, but almost too late. For us, it can make a difference right now. The Sacrament of Reconciliation is not just coming here, confessing our sins, receiving absolution and then going home. It also involves repentance, conversion, change.

When we walk out of here today, we have to be different people than when we came in. This will happen if we let the graces we receive in this Sacrament change us in the ways we need to change. We'll stop doing things we know are wrong. We'll do more of the things we know are good. We'll pray more. We'll come to church more. We'll share more of our blessings, do more for others. We'll forgive more. We'll say "I'm sorry" more. We'll care more and do more about injustices in the world. We'll love more. This is the work of repentance that we must commit ourselves to. Otherwise, this Sacrament is meaningless. Now we won't do it perfectly; we never do. That's OK. The important thing is that this time we try harder. That's all God asks of us. And when we do, when we do, it'll be as if we are looking into the eyes of our crucified Savior and saying, "Thank you, Jesus, thank you." AMEN.

CONNECTING TO THE WORD

1. Why do you think Bob continued to reach out to Rusty? What finally helped Rusty to hear what Bob was trying to tell him?

2. What did Bob give to Rusty? What did Rusty give to Bob?

3. Have you ever been a Bob to a Rusty or a Rusty to a Bob? If so, reflect on how you might have been changed by the experience.

4. What do you think Rusty meant when he said he was finally going to have a home? Have you ever felt spiritually "at home"? Have you ever felt spiritually "homeless"? How do you feel now?

5. Is it possible for us to shelter another in God's love prior to our last breath on earth? How difficult would it be for you to be like Bob for another person?

6. What do you believe in your heart about God's capacity to forgive? Do you have a hard time accepting God's mercy for yourself? Do you have a hard time accepting God's mercy for others, especially those — like Rusty — who have committed very serious sins, and come to God only in the last hour?

7. Can you imagine any better way that God could have shown His great love for us than to become one of us in Jesus and suffer and die for our sins?

RECONCILATION SERVICE

Luke 15:1-3, 11-24

Arms Open Wide!

Father Albert Shamon who wrote a regular column for the *Catholic Courier* told a story about a widow who had lost her husband and her only son during World War I. She was devastated by her loss and was very bitter, especially since one of her neighbors had seen five sons go to war, and they had all come back. One night the grieving widow cried herself to sleep, and she had a dream. An angel appeared before her and said, "You can have your son back to relive any twenty minutes of his life. What twenty minutes would you choose?" The mother thought for a few moments. Would she have him back as a baby in her arms, or as a dirty-faced little toddler, or a little boy just starting school, or maybe as a student just graduating from high school, or as the young soldier who so bravely marched off to war? Finally she told the angel, "Let me have him back that time as a little boy, when he got really angry at me and he doubled up his little fists and shook them at me and said, 'I hate you, momma, I hate you!'"

The angel asked her why she chose such an unpleasant time, and the mother explained, "Because, right after that, his anger subsided and he came back to me, tears streaming down his grimy little face, and he put his arms around me and said, 'Momma, I'm sorry I was so naughty. I promise never to be bad again, and I really, really love you.'... Please, let me have him back for those twenty minutes, because I never loved him more than at that moment when he came back to me."

Whether we're parents or not, if we can identify with the feelings of the mother in this story, or the feelings of the father in Jesus' parable in today's Gospel, we can begin to grasp exactly how God feels about each of His children. God never loves us more than when we come back to Him after being away; not "away" in a physical sense, but spiritually. Sin pushes us away from our infinitely good, infinitely holy God. Everything we do that is contrary to God's vision for us — God's dream for us — drives us further away. Every time we fail to love each other with the same love God has for us, the distance grows greater and greater. Just like in these two stories, it is the pain of separation, and our recognition that our sins have caused this separation, that brings some of us here today. If we've come here with genuine sorrow and repentance in our heart, if we are ready to acknowledge and confess our failures, ready to amend our lives, then the Father who loves and cares for us in spite of our failures, the Father whose grace is greatest when we are weakest, is here and ready to welcome us back. He's ready to give us the Good News that our failures are not fatal. We are forgiven.

And not only are we forgiven, but our sins are taken away, erased, just as if they were never there. They are washed away — washed away in the blood of Christ, the sacrificial lamb of God. They are forgotten. We can thank Jesus Christ for God's short memory, for making it possible for us to leave this church today as saints after coming in as sinners.

Yet, I wonder if there may be some of us here who are not too sure about all of this — not too sure about where we stand with God. Some of you might be thinking, "I have really messed up; I just can't see how God can ever forgive and forget." Or maybe you can't bring yourself to promise God that you will make the changes He wants you to make to get your life on track because you're afraid you'll fall back into those same old patterns. Maybe you're just not convinced that God can really love you as you are right now.

I would bet that the prodigal son in our Gospel story experienced some of these same doubts and fears as he made that long walk back home. The road home must have seemed a lot longer and rougher than he remembered. As he walked along he kept rehearsing what he would say to his father: "Father, I have sinned against heaven and against you, I no longer deserve to be called your son." How different these words were from the ones he used when he had demanded his share of his father's wealth. He was going home a changed man. His defiance had been replaced with sorrow and remorse.

But as he approached the road that led up to the house, his plan to go home suddenly didn't seem like such a good idea. He could remember the look of hurt on his father's face when he had told him he was leaving. And he knew that the stories about his loose and lavish lifestyle must've gotten back to his father. "What's the use?" he must've thought. "I really blew it. How can I expect my father to forgive me?" He had no idea how much his father had missed him and longed for him to come back. He was about to turn around and walk away, when he spotted a figure running toward him. When the figure got closer he could see that it was his father — tears running down his cheeks, arms stretched from east to west welcoming his son home..."Father I have sinned." The rest of the words were muffled as the boy buried his face into his father's shoulder. Words were not necessary. Repentance had been made; forgiveness had been given. He was home.

When Jesus told this parable of the loving father, I wonder, did He use his hands when he got to this part of the story. Did He open his arms wide to illustrate the point? Did He sense that there were some in his audience of sinners and outcasts who were thinking, "I could never go home, not after what I've done. I can't start over." And did He open His arms even wider as if to say, "Yes, yes you can. You can come home."?

Whether he opened His arms that day or not, we don't know. But we do know that He did later. He stretched His hands open as far as He could. He forced His arms so wide apart that it hurt. And to prove that those arms and hands would never be closed to us, He had them nailed open. And they still are.[1] AMEN.

CONNECTING TO THE WORD

1. Can you recall a time in your life when someone who was estranged from you came back ? If so, do you remember how you felt at the time? Compare your feelings to those of the mother and the father in our two stories.

2. Do you believe that we can push ourselves so far away from God that we can never go back? Have you ever felt that way? If so, what made you realize that God was waiting to welcome you back?

3. Do you believe that God loves you just as you are right now? Do you think He would love you more if you were a better person? Would He love you less if you were a worse person?

4. Do you have things in your life right now that are creating a distance between you and God? If so, are you – like the Prodigal Son – willing to do what it takes to change those things and "come home"?

NOTES

1. The ending for this homily is drawn from Max Lucado, *Six Hours One Friday* (Portland, Oregon: Multnomah, 1989), 114-115.

PASSION SUNDAY – YEAR B

Mark 14:1 – 15:47

It Will All Turn Out Right

People sometimes ask me, "Where do you get ideas for your homilies?" I usually answer that I hope they come from God, but I'm not always sure. Sometimes, though, there's no doubt that God has a hand in it. Like last week. I was really struggling over what to preach about today, and I had been praying day after day, "Lord, it's Palm Sunday; there'll be so many people there. Come on, tell me the message you want them to hear." But nothing came. I guess I just wasn't tuned in to His answer. Until a last minute phone call made me late for Mass one weekday morning. Since I was late, I sat in one of the back pews instead of the front pew where I usually do... When I came back to my seat after communion, I started thinking again about today's homily and I looked up at the figure of Jesus hanging on the cross — something I couldn't have done if I had been sitting in my usual place.

I focused on His eyes, those eyes that seem to be expressing all of the pain and suffering of the world. Then, for some reason I can't explain, I followed the direction those pain-filled eyes seemed to be looking in, and they appeared to be looking right at this young girl — on her knees, her head buried in her hands, deep in prayer. I knew she was hurting; a few days earlier I had prayed over her because she was in the grip of a serious and frightening illness. For the next few moments, my eyes were glued to this scene of the suffering Jesus looking down at His precious, suffering child. My heart ached for her as I imagined her pleading with God in words something like these: "God, why is this happening to me ? I've tried so hard to be a good kid. Can't you make this go away ? Why do I have to go through this?"

It reminded me of the scene we just heard in the Garden of Gethsemane: God looking down at His precious Son, Jesus, praying in agony, asking to be spared from the horrible punishment and death he could see coming. During those hours of anguished prayer, Jesus must have said more than those few words recorded in the Gospels. Maybe He said something like this: "Father, why does this have to happen? I've tried to do everything you asked of me. Is my suffering and dying going to make any difference? Do I have to go through with this plan of yours? Isn't there some other way ?"

That young girl was having her own Gethsemane experience. Sooner or later, everyone of us will have a Gethsemane experience — that time when something totally outside our choosing happens, or is about to happen, to us or someone we care about, something we would just as soon pass us by. And we come to God on our knees begging, pleading, "Lord, can't you take this away?" And Jesus looks down at us from the cross and His eyes speak to us — just as they spoke to her that morning: "I know what you are going through... I've been there. I've been where you are. I'm not going to tell you it will be easy. It won't. But if you trust the Father - as I did - it will all turn out right."

Yes, at Gethsemane, despite all His human fears and doubts, Jesus chose to trust His Father: "Not my will, but yours, be done (Luke 22:42)." Jesus could've turned His back on the whole mess and gone away, but He didn't. He walked the path His Father chose for Him to walk; He drank from the cup His Father gave him to drink, and in the end, it all turned out right... Death was turned into glorious new life; ugliness was transformed into beauty, tragedy into triumph... And that's what Jesus wants us to do — place our trust in the Father's love as we sweat and pray through our own Gethsemanes — the big ones and the small ones, whether we're nine or ninety. Take the path the Father chooses for us, drink from the cup He gives us to drink, and Jesus promises that it will all turn out right. It may take longer than we would like. It may not happen the way we expected. But it will happen. That's the promise of Easter. That's the promise of the empty tomb. That's the promise Christ sealed for us with His precious blood. AMEN.

CONNECTING TO THE WORD

1. Have your plans for your life ever clashed with God's will for your life? How did you become aware of this discordance? Did you continue to reject God's plan? Are you still clashing against it? Or have you been open to letting God work His divine plan, at His pace, into the rhythm of your life?

2. Have you had a Gethsemane experience? Was dropping to your knees and asking for God's help a last resort tactic? What message, if any, did you receive? How did your Gethsemane turn out? How did you get through it ?

3. Do you know someone who is going through a Gethsemane experience right now? How might you help them get through it? What can you tell them from your own experiences that could give them hope?

GOOD FRIDAY

*Isaiah 52:13-53:12; Hebrews 4:14-16, 5:7-9;
John 18:1-19:42*

Under His Wings

"It is finished."… In John's version of Our Lord's Passion, these are the last words Jesus utters before giving up His spirit. "It is finished." Is this a cry of defeat? Is this an admission of failure? No! It is a declaration of triumph — of victory. Jesus had accomplished the mission His Father had sent Him to do, and now His work on earth is finished, completed, ended. His work, His mission had been foretold by the prophet Isaiah. Listen again to the words from our first reading as Isaiah speaks of the Messiah as suffering servant: "He was pierced for our offenses, crushed for our sins; upon him was the punishment that makes us whole; … We had all gone astray… but the Lord laid upon him the guilt of us all… Through his suffering… their guilt he shall bear… And he shall take away the sins of many, and win pardon for their offenses."

These are words that we dare not forget on this day of Jesus' death, nor on any day of our Christian lives, because they remind us that the suffering and pain and anguish Jesus endured, were all for us, for our offenses, our sins, our guilt. Without his suffering and death, we would have to pay the price for ourselves; and that price would be eternal separation from God — in other words, hell. That's what hell is — being forever separated from God, from all that is good, all that is holy, all that is love. Without Jesus' sacrificial love we would be doomed to an eternity without God .

A penetrating picture of sacrificial love appeared in an article in National Geographic several years ago. The article describes the aftermath of a forest fire in Yellowstone National Park. Forest rangers had begun their climb up a mountain to assess the fire's damage. As they surveyed the devastation, a ranger stumbled upon an eerie sight. He found the body of a bird that was literally petrified in ashes; it was perched like a statue on the ground near the base of a tree. He poked at the bird with a stick and knocked it over. And all of a sudden three tiny chicks scurried out from under their dead mother's wings... three tiny chicks.

That loving mother apparently had seen the impending disaster coming, and instinctively she must have known that the toxic smoke would rise, so she had carried her babies to the base of the tree. And there she gathered them safely under her wings. She could have saved herself — flown to safety, away from the dangerous fire — but she refused to abandon her chicks. When the blaze arrived and the heat engulfed her own body, she had remained there steadfast, protecting their tiny bodies from the scorching heat. Because she had been willing to die, those little ones under the cover of her wings would live.

Because Jesus had been willing to die, those under the cover of His wings would live. That night in the garden, Jesus had been keenly aware of the impending disaster. John tells us that Jesus knew everything that was going to happen to Him. There in the garden as He prayed and agonized, Jesus could see what was coming. *He saw how they would put Him on trial and falsely accuse Him, how the crowds would condemn Him to die. He saw how they would strip and whip Him mercilessly, how they would mockingly crown Him king…They would drag Him up that hill to Calvary, force Him to carry that heavy cross, pound long metal spikes into His hands and feet. There He would hang on that cross and die in the most horrible way imaginable — pain searing through every bone, every muscle, choking to death on His own breath… Jesus knew what was coming.*

Yet like that mother bird, Jesus refused to fly away, refused to run away and save Himself. He could've, but out of loving obedience to His Father, and out of His incredible love for us, He remained steadfast in carrying out God's plan for our salvation: "Not my will, but yours be done."

On that burning mountain, that mother bird had spread her wings and sheltered her children to save them from the ravages of fire… On that angry hill, God had spread open His arms and let them be nailed to a tree, to save His children from the ravages of sin.

And that, my friends, is why today — Friday — is *Good* Friday. It is good for us. It is the best thing that could ever have happened to us. We believe this; that's why we're here. But has it made any difference in our lives? Are we going to let another Lent come and go without responding in some concrete way to the Love that was poured out for us on Calvary? Do we understand that when Jesus declared, "It is finished!", it was actually just the beginning for us? His mission then became our mission — all of us who call ourselves Christians. Before he died, Jesus commanded His followers to "love one another as I have loved you," because he knew that transforming the world — breaking the cycle of hatred, selfishness, greed, and intolerance — had to start with each individual heart. It had to start with you and me loving as we have never loved before, as He loved us: loving without looking at what's in it for us; loving those we don't like very much; loving the ones who hate us, who hurt us, who won't love us in return (anybody can love someone who loves them back); loving when it costs us — no matter how much.

And so, in a few moments, as we come forward to touch or kiss or kneel at the foot of the cross, let's try to really feel the love that radiates from that cross, and let that love so fill our hearts that it spills over into every corner of our everyday world: where we live, where we work, where we go to school, where we play, or shop, or just hang out; every place that LOVE needs to be.

Then, when we come to that final moment, as we're breathing our last breath, knowing that we have tried to be all Jesus asked us to be, we will be able to say to the Father, "It is finished!", and we'll know — as Jesus did — that for us it is not really the end. It is just the beginning. AMEN.

CONNECTING TO THE WORD

1. How can we break the cycle of hatred, selfishness, greed, and intolerance on earth so as to avoid creating hell on earth? Has a state of disconnectedness from God and loved ones placed you in a hell on earth?

2. If you have known separation from God or love, have you since become reconnected? How did you do this? How did the quality of your life and the lives of those around you change? Is it possible to, through love, create heaven on earth?

3. Who would you be willing to shelter with your wings? Have you ever sheltered someone with your wings? Has someone ever sheltered you with their wings? How did it feel?

4. What is a mission on earth that you would not abandon or fly away from if you were faced with adversity? Have you ever been faced with adversity and flown away? Why? What connections would have caused you or helped you to stay? Have you ever stayed when it would be easier to go? What was the source of strength that gave you courage to stay?

5. In what ways are endings really beginnings? Reflect on a joyous ending such as a graduation and a sad ending such as death. How are they different? How are they similar? How does love

and support help us to arrive at a graduation? How does love and support help us to move on after the death of a loved one?

THEME INDEX

THEME	HOMILIES CONTAINING THIS THEME
Compassion	Sixth Sunday, Ordinary-B
Conversion	Third Sunday, Advent-A
	Lenten Penance Service
Divorce	Twenty-seventh Sunday, Ordinary-A
Eucharist	Tenth Sunday, Ordinary-A
	Body and Blood of Christ, Year C
Faith	Thirty-second Sunday, Ordinary-A
	Twenty-seventh Sunday, Ordinary-C
Familial Love	Twenty-seventh Sunday, Ordinary-A
Final Judgment	Thirtieth Sunday, Ordinary-A
	Christ the King – A
Following Jesus	Third Sunday, Lent-A
	Second Sunday, Lent-C
	Twenty-first Sunday, Ordinary-C
Forgiveness	Second Sunday, Ordinary-A
	Lenten Penance Service

THEME	HOMILIES CONTAINING THIS THEME
God the Father	Fifth Sunday, Easter-A
God, Triune	Trinity Sunday, Year-C
Guilt	Reconciliation Service
Happiness	Third Sunday, Advent-C
Heaven, Hell	Twenty-first Sunday, Ordinary-C
	All Soul's Day
Human Dignity	Twenty-second Sunday, Ordinary-C
	Twenty-ninth Sunday, Ordinary-C
Jesus, Gethsemane	Passion Sunday – Year B
Jesus on the Cross	Good Friday
Jesus' Love For Us	Good Friday
Joy	Third Sunday, Advent-C
Justice, Biblical	Twenty-ninth Sunday, Ordinary-C
Knowing Jesus	Second Sunday, Ordinary-B
Lamb of God	Second Sunday, Ordinary-A
Light of Christ	Fifth Sunday, Ordinary-A
Light of Faith	Fifth Sunday, Ordinary-A

THEME	HOMILIES CONTAINING THIS THEME
Putting Christ First	Second Sunday, Ordinary-B
Real Presence	Tenth Sunday, Ordinary-A
Reconciliation	Lenten Penance Service Reconciliation Service
Repentance	Second Sunday, Advent-A Second Sunday, Ordinary-A Lenten Penance Service
Respect for Life	Twenty-seventh Sunday, Ordinary-C
Salvation	Twenty-first Sunday, Ordinary-C
Showing God to Others	Fifth Sunday, Easter-A
Sin	Second Sunday, Ordinary-A
Social Justice	Twenty-ninth Sunday, Ordinary-C
Solitude	Sixteenth Sunday, Ordinary-B;
Trinity, Holy	Trinity Sunday – Year C
Troubles and Sorrows	Fourth Sunday, Ordinary-A
Trust in God	Thirty-second Sunday, Ordinary-A

THEME	HOMILIES CONTAINING THIS THEME
Truth of Christ	Fourth Sunday, Ordinary-C
Word of God Words, Power of	Third Sunday, Lent-A Eighth Sunday, Ordinary-C

Printed in the United States
60916LVS00001B/52-102